DUE

JOHN LOCKE AND THE DOCTRINE OF MAJORITY-RULE

UNIVERSITY OF ILLINOIS PRESS, URBANA, 1965

JOHN LOCKE
AND THE DOCTRINE
OF MAJORITY-RULE

WILLMOORE KENDALL

Originally published as Vol. 26, No. 2, in the Illinois Studies in the Social Sciences.

Manufactured in the United States of America. Library of Congress Catalog Card No. 41-52730.

CONTENTS

———

ACKNOWLEDGMENT

THE PRESENT STUDY was planned, and the relevant investigation begun, under the direction of the late James Wilford Garner, to whom—on this as on many other counts—the writer owes a profound debt of gratitude. He only wishes that the following pages might have been worthy of the scholarly tradition which Professor Garner bequeathed to his department at the University of Illinois.

After Professor Garner's untimely death, Professor John A. Fairlie generously agreed to accept directorial responsibility for the project, as, when it became evident that Professor Fairlie would be absent from Urbana during the last crucial weeks of actual writing, Professor Francis G. Wilson amiably consented to give the writer the benefit of his erudition and critical acumen. To both of them, alike for the indulgent patience with which they have witnessed his tergiversations and for the keen criticism with which they have on numerous occasions come to his rescue, he is deeply grateful.

PART ONE

INTRODUCTION

CHAPTER I

PRELIMINARY CONSIDERATIONS ON THE DOCTRINE OF MAJORITY-RULE

SPECULATION about the political rôle of majorities is as old as Western political theory. "Democrats," says Aristotle in the *Politics*, "say that justice is that to which the majority agree, oligarchs that to which the wealthier class; in their [the oligarchs'] opinion the decision should be given according to the amount of property. In both principles there is some inequality and some injustice."[1] Elsewhere he writes:

The principle that the multitude ought to be supreme rather than the few best is *one that is maintained,* and though not free from difficulty, yet seems to contain an element of truth. For the many, of whom each individual is but an ordinary person, when they meet together may very likely be better than the few good, if regarded not individually but collectively, just as a feast to which many contribute is better than a dinner provided out of a single purse. For each individual among the many has a share of virtue and prudence, and when they meet together, they become in a manner one man. . . . Some understand one part, and some another, and among them they understand the whole.[2]

Aristotle's great teacher, who had, of course, an understandable grievance against majorities, returns to the problem again and again in his dialogues; and, like many modern writers, identifies majority-rule with majority-tyranny:

Imagine then a fleet or a ship in which there is a captain who is taller and stronger than any of the crew, but he is a little deaf and has a similar infirmity in sight, and his knowledge of navigation is not much better. Now the sailors are quarrelling with one another about the steering; every one is of the opinion that he ought to steer, though he has never learned and cannot tell who taught him or when he learned, and will even assert that the art of navigation cannot be taught, and is ready to cut in pieces him who says the contrary. They throng about the captain, and do all they can to make him commit the helm to them; and if he refuses them and others prevail, they kill the others or throw them overboard, and having first

---

[1]Aristotle, *Politica* (translated by Benjamin Jowett), vi. 3. 1318a.
[2]*Ibid.*, iii. 11. 1281a-b (italics mine). Passages of this kind from Aristotle must, of course, be handled gingerly, alike because of Aristotle's habit of paraphrasing current opinions which he did not share, and because he almost certainly means by the multitude (= majority?) the majority of the people *not counting women, metics, or slaves.* Aristotle's "better" opinion probably reveals itself in such a passage as the following: "Now they agree in saying that whatever is decided by a majority of the *citizens* is to be deemed law. Granted:—but not without some reserve; since there are two classes out of which a state is composed,—the poor and the rich,— that is to be deemed law, on which both or the greater part of both agree; and if they disagree, that which is approved by the greater number, and by those who have the higher qualification" (*ibid.*, vi. 3. 1318a, italics mine). (Query: Aristotle the first proponent of a system of concurrent majorities?) But cf. *ibid.*, iii. 15. 1286a: "The state is made up of many individuals. And as a feast to which all the guests contribute is better than a banquet furnished by a single man, so a multitude is a better judge of many things than any individual. Again, the many are more incorruptible than the few; they are like the greater quantity of water which is less easily corrupted than a little. The individual is liable to be overcome by anger or by some other passion, and then his judgement is necessarily perverted; but it is hardly to be supposed that a great number of persons would all get into a passion and go wrong at the same moment." Apparently Aristotle was of two minds on this issue, and Catlin might well qualify such a statement as the following: "Why the *majority* will alone—that of the numerical majority—should be the index of the General Will is a question not so much answered by Rousseau as brusqued. It is, we are given to understand—contrary to the opinion . . . . of Aristotle . . . . the best practical way" (*The Story of the Political Philosophers* [New York: McGraw-Hill Book Co., 1939], p. 454).

chained up the noble captain's senses with drink or some narcotic drug, they
mutiny and take possession of the ship and make themselves at home with the
stores; and thus, eating and drinking, they continue their voyage with such success
as might be expected of them.[3]

Again like the modern critics of majority-rule, he believes that it results
inevitably in the substitution of demagogues for statesmen:

Him who is their partisan and zealous in the design of getting the ship out of
the captain's hand into their own, whether by force or persuasion, they compliment
with the name of sailor, pilot, able seaman, and abuse the other sort of man
and call him good-for-nothing; but they have not even a notion that the true
pilot must pay attention to the year and seasons and sky and stars and winds, and
whatever else belongs to his art, if he intends to be really qualified for the command of the ship; while at the same time he must and will be the steerer, *whether
other people like or not. . . .*[4]

Indeed, Plato is almost ready to say that where moral judgments are
concerned the many are necessarily wrong:

In questions of just and unjust, fair and foul, good and evil, which are the subjects of our present consultation, ought we to follow the opinion of the many
and to fear them; or the opinion of the one man who has understanding? . . . .
You begin in error when you advise that we should regard the opinion of the
many about just and unjust, good and evil, honourable and dishonourable.[5]

And, though he certainly believed that governments ought to rule in the
interests of all rather than in the interests of a single class,[6] it is into
the mouth of Protagoras that he puts the words which would turn such
a concession into an argument for governments subject to popular control:

Hermes asked Zeus how he should impart justice and reverence among men:—
should he distribute them as the arts are distributed; that is to say, to a favoured
few only, one skilled individual having enough of medicine or of any other art
for many unskilled ones? Shall this be the manner in which I distribute justice
and reverence among men, or shall I give them to all? To all, said Zeus; I should
like them all to have a share; for cities cannot exist, if a few only share in the
virtues, as in the arts.[7]

The proposition that there is resident in the majority a certain virtue
which, outweighing all the claims of expertise or intellectual superiority,
gives it the right to make final decisions affecting the welfare of the state,

---

[3]Plato, *Republic* (translated by Benjamin Jowett), vi. 488.

[4]*Ibid.* (italics mine). The latter part of this passage is translated quite differently by Paul
Shorey in his edition of the *Republic* in the Loeb Classical Library (London: William Heinemann, 2 vols., 1930-1935), but the variations do not impair its applicability in the connection in
which we have used it.

[5]Plato, *Crito*, 47-48. Cf. *Laws*, i. 627: "Citizens who . . . . live in the same cities, may
unjustly conspire, and having the superiority in numbers may overcome and enslave the few
just; and when they prevail, the state may be truly called its own inferior and therefore bad;
and when they are defeated, superior and therefore good." It is interesting to note that Plato,
anticipating an important modern tendency in political thought, believed it was possible to escape
between the horns of the dilemma, majority-rule versus minority-rule: "Now, which would be
the better judge,—one who destroyed the bad and required the good to govern themselves; or
one who, while allowing the good to govern, let the bad live, and made them voluntarily submit?
Or lastly, there might be a third excellent judge who . . . . not only did not destroy anyone, but
reconciled them to one another for ever after, and *gave them laws which they mutually observed,
and was able to keep them friends*" (*ibid.*, 627-8, italics mine). See below, pp. 19-21.

[6]Plato, *Republic*, iv. 420. Wherefore obedience, as he argues elsewhere, is due only to the
ruler who uses his power in the interests of his subjects (*ibid.*, i. 342).

[7]Plato, *Protagoras*, 322. Protagoras continues: "And this is the reason, Socrates, why the
Athenians and mankind in general, when the question relates to . . . . political virtue, which
proceeds only by way of justice and wisdom, ... are patient enough of any man who speaks
of them, as is also natural, because they think that every man ought to share in this sort of
virtue, and that states could not exist if this were otherwise" (*ibid.*, 322-323).

was more or less a commonplace in the utterances of the democratic statesmen of the ancient world. Thus, for example, the leader of the popular party at Syracuse, Athenagoras, maintained that although "the wise [are] the best counsellors, ... the many, when they have heard a matter discussed, [are] the best judges."[8] And even at Rome it was necessary for Claudius, at the moment that he was deliberating measures to nullify the will of a majority, to concede that adequate guarantees of free speech justify the majority-principle:

Aequum enim est, ut unusquisque declaret, quae e republica fore existimat, sed pareat iis, quae a pluribus fuerint decreta.[9]

While there is ample evidence that political theory took cognizance of the problem of majority-rule not only in Classical antiquity but repeatedly through the intervening period,[10] it was not until the late seventeenth and

[8]Thucydides (translated by Benjamin Jowett), vi. 39. In the light of what we shall argue below (p. 122), it is interesting to observe that Athenagoras believes that where the rich are first heard on matters of finance and the wise on matters of general policy, the majority subsequently making the decision, the result is equality for all. On the capacity of the majority to make decisions, cf. the declaration of Pericles in his famous eulogy of Athenian democracy: "If few of us are originators, we are all sound judges of a policy" (*ibid.*, i. 40).

[9]Dionysius of Halicarnassus, *Antiquitates Romanae* (translated by J. J. Reiske), xi. 56.

[10]Cf. Otto von Gierke, "Über die Geschichte des Majoritätsprinzipes," *Schmollers Jahrbuch für Gesetzgebung, Verwaltung und Volkswirtschaft im Deutschen Reiche*, XXXIX (1915), p. 566: "In der griechischen Staatslehre stossen wir überhaupt nicht auf Reflexionen über den Grund der Geltung des Stimmenmehrs. Erst die römischen Juristen suchen nach dem Geltungsgrunde. Sie begnügen sich aber mit einer sehr äusserlichen Rechtfertigung." Cf. Joseph Stawski, *Le principe de la majorité* (Gedani: Ex Officina Boenigiana, 1920), p. 73: "L'évolution des idées juridiques sur le principe de la majorité sera déterminée par le développement des conceptions au sujet des corporations, en particulier, des décisions corporatives. Réaliser ce progrès sera l'œuvre de la science juridique du moyen-âge." The following lines are from the younger Pliny (*Epistolae*, ii. 12): "Sed hoc pluribus visum est. Numerantur enim sententiae, non ponderantur; nec aliud in publico consilio potest fieri, in quo nihil est tam inaequale quam aequalitat ipsa: nam cum sit impar prudentia, par omnium ius est." Both Ulpian and Scaevola stated in the clearest manner possible the central notion involved in majority-rule, but they are, be it noted, merely setting down a *legal rule*, and are not expressing an opinion as to whether or not it is a wise or useful one. Thus Ulpian (*ap.* Gierke, *loc. cit.*): "Refertur ad universos, quod publice fit per majorem partem"; and Scaevola (*ibid.*): "Quod major pars curiae effecit pro eo habetur, ac si omnes egerint." Cf. Edoardo Ruffini Avondo, *Il principio maggioritario* (Torino: Fratelli Bocca, 1927), pp. 21-22: "Bandita ogni ricerca sulla sua opportunità politica e sul suo valore morale, i Romani si preoccuparono anzitutto di dargli [il principio maggioritario] una formulazione giuridicamente esatta, classificandolo nel quadro dei fenomeni giuridici." The belief that Marsilius of Padua's dictum (*Defensor pacis* [Leipzig and Berlin: Verlag von B. G. Teubner, 1914], i. 12. 3) that "legislatorem seu causam legis effectivam primam et propriam esse populum seu civium universitatem, aut eius valentiorem partem per suam electionem seu voluntatem in generali civium congregatione per sermonem expressam, praecipientem seu determinantem aliquid fieri vel omitti circa civiles actus humanos sub poena vel supplicio temporali: valentiorem inquam partem, considerata quantitate in communitate illa super quam lex fertur; sive id fecerit universitas praedicta civium aut eius pars valentior per seipsam immediate, sive id alicui vel aliquibus commiserit faciendum, qui legislator simpliciter non sunt nec esse possunt, sed solum ad aliquid et quandoque, ac secundum primi legislatoris auctoritatem," stamps him as an ally of the majority-rule democrats, is now in disrepute. See C. H. McIlwain, *The Growth of Political Thought in the West* (New York: The Macmillan Co., 1932), pp. 303-304, where current misapprehensions regarding Marsilius' position are attributed to the omission of the words "et qualitate" from all the texts of the *Defensor pacis* printed before 1928. (In C. W. Previté-Orton's critical edition [Cambridge: University Press, 1928] the words "considerata quantitate" of the foregoing quotation are followed by "personarum et qualitate.") The quotation from Marsilius is, nevertheless, evidence that the idea of majority-rule had not been forgotten (Marsilius having at least taken the care to dissociate himself from it), and is thus relevant here. It in fact identified him with the canon law doctrine that decisions should be made by the *maior et sanior pars*, which, according to Stawski (*op. cit.*, p. 76), was less a denial that there existed a presumption in favor of the opinion of the *pars numerosior* than an insistence that the latter must go by the board when such presumption is refuted. Cf. Ruffini Avondo, *op. cit.*, pp. 31-32: "La maggioranza numerica è anche la parte più sana del collegio, salvo prova contraria. L'onere della prova spettava alla minoranza." The same writer summarizes (*ibid.*) an earlier form of the doctrine of *sanioritas* as follows: "Quando la minoranza supera in zelo, autorità e dignità la maggioranza, quest' ultima soccombe, dovendosi i più chiamare i meno, e i meno chiamare i più." After Marsilius, writes J. G. Heinberg ("Theories of Majority Rule," *American Political Science Review*, XXVI [June, 1932], p. 457), "we find the dogma of majority rule a prominent, although never explicitly and thoroughly developed, part of the current political theory." Cf. Hugo Grotius, *De iure belli ac pacis libri tres* (Lugduni Batavorum: Apud A. W. Sijthoff, 1919), ii. 5. 17: "Consociationes praeter hanc maxime naturalem sunt et aliae, tum privatae, tum publicae: et hae quidem aut in populum, aut ex populis. Habent autem omnes hoc commune,

eighteenth centuries (after 1688 and, if not the birth, at least the conception of the first of the great modern democracies) that it came into
its own.[11] It came into its own, as political problems often do, after it
had been posed more or less clearly in practice;[12] for even those who
most strenuously deny the identity between majority-rule and democracy
will no doubt agree that *one* of the problems suggested by the events of
1688[13] was that of the claims of a majority (in this case, to be sure, a
very large majority) of an established community to name the conditions upon which it is willing to participate in a common social adventure with persons (or, in *our* language, with a minority) who conceive
that adventure in terms different from its own. In 1688 the minority
"acquiesced," wherefore Englishmen can call the revolution which occurred in that year the Bloodless Revolution. This was well; but it
meant, among other things, that opinions might subsequently differ as to
what had happened. The minority having peacefully acquiesced, there
was a presumption that the majority had pressed its claims "responsibly,"
and had named conditions less severe than it might have but for its
recognition of a limit upon the validity of those claims. On the other
hand, this was only a presumption. The minority had indeed acquiesced,
but perhaps it had done so by necessity rather than by choice. Perhaps
the Settlement did represent the full measure of what the majority cared
to demand. In short, though History had posed a problem, none could
with authority say that he had read aright the question she had asked.

In this sense, but only in this sense, political theory proceeded to get
ahead of history for a time; and the problem to which Locke in 1690
devoted his *Second Treatise* did not present itself in *unambiguous* historical form until 1776 or 1789. Even 1776 is doubtful—here again because
men can read differently the meaning of what happened. Burke could
argue, alike with regard to 1776[14] and 1688[15] that the majority, very far

---

quod in iis rebus ob quas consociatio quaeque instituta est, universitas, et eius pars maior
nomine universitatis obligant singulos qui sunt in societate. Omnino enim ea credenda est fuisse
voluntas in societatem coëuntium, ut ratio aliqua esset expediendi negotia: est autem manifeste
iniquum, ut pars maior sequatur minorem: quare naturaliter, seclusis pactis ac legibus quae
formam tractandis negotiis imponunt, pars maior ius habet integri." Cf. Thomas Hobbes,
Elementa philosophica de cive (Amsterodami: Apud L. & D. Elzevirios, 1657), vi. 2: "Consideran-
dum deinde est, unumquemque ex multitudine (quo constituendae civitatis principium fiat) debere
consentire cum caeteris ut in iis rebus quae a quopiam in coetu proponentur, pro voluntate
omnium habeatur id, quod voluerit eorum major pars." Cf. Samuel Pufendorf, *De officio hominis
et civis juxte legem naturalem libri duo* (New York: Oxford University Press, 1927), ii. 6. 12:
"Verum ubi regimen civitatis collatum est in concilium, ex pluribus hominibus constans, quorum
quisque suam retinet voluntatem naturalem; regulariter illud habetur pro voluntate civitatis, in
quod consenserit *major pars* hominum, ex quibus concilium componitur."

[11]Wolodymyr Starosolskyj, *Das Majoritätsprinzip* (Wien: F. Deuticke, 1916), p. 6: "Das
Ende des XVIII. Jahrhunderts bildet die wichtigste Epoche in der Geschichte des Majoritätsprinzips. Die Lehren des Naturrechts über die Natürlichkeit und Wichtigkeit des Prinzips
haben in der grossen französischen Revolution ihren praktischen Ausdruck gefunden."

[12]*Ibid.*, p. 35: "Es ist eine Erscheinung von grosser Bedeutung, dass die Erörterung der
Frage nach der Zweckmässigkeit der sozialen Institutionen und die Versuche, sie zu rechtfertigen,
diesen Institutionen historisch nicht vorangehen, sondern ihnen nachfolgen."

[13]So also by those of the Protectorate, where, however, the heterogeneity of the Cromwellian
movement finally prevented the issue from being posed in terms of majority vs. minority.

[14]Edmund Burke, "An Appeal from the New to the Old Whigs," *Works* (London: Henry
G. Bohn, 1855), III, p. 31.

[15]*Ibid.*, pp. 44-45.

from asserting a right to determine unilaterally the conditions upon which the society might continue in existence, was (in a case of *absolute neces-sity*) merely holding the minority to conditions previously agreed. *Pacta sunt servanda*, and no foolishness about a majority-principle! Similarly, the authors of the new constitution of the United States either saw no majority-rule implications in the events through which they had been living, or (if they did see such implications) studiously avoided pointing them up in the new frame of government. The Tory minority which had taken refuge in Canada, on the other hand, may well have felt—when news came to them a few years later of the turn things had taken in France—that History was repeating itself; and majority-rule democrats can always point to our elaborate system of checks and balances as evi-dence that even the constitution-makers of Philadelphia were sufficiently aware of History's having posed a question about majority-rule to answer it in the negative.

Whatever the correct conclusion may be with regard to 1776, there seems to be no doubt about 1789. Here the minority were not even in-vited to acquiesce, and the majority, *i.e.*, the leaders of the majority, wasted no words upon talk of ancient agreements. They were, rather, in-clined to insist upon the novelty of the principles on which they were acting: They did what they did because they were the majority, and the majority does not need to name reasons for what it does. "La loi," they wrote solemnly into their constitution, "est la volonté générale, exprimée par la majorité ou des citoyens ou de leurs représentants."[16] The Abbé Sieyès was hardly willing to discuss the question; the principle of ma-jority-rule had been "demonstrated," and was, presumably, no more open to challenge than the laws of geometry:

Nous avons démontré la nécessité de ne reconnaître la volonté commune que dans l'avis de la pluralité. *Cette maxime est incontestable.*[17]

Mirabeau had a ready answer for those who saw in the principle the possibility of "one-man" decisions, and could accuse them of timidity:

Ceux qui s'opposent à cette loi sont séduits par l'espèce de frayeur que leur cause l'idée de voir la prépondérance d'un seul suffrage décider *les questions les plus importantes*. Mais qu'ils ne s'y trompent pas; ce n'est pas tel ou tel suffrage qui décide, c'est la comparaison de la somme de ceux qui disent *oui*, avec la somme de ceux qui disent *non*.[18]

It was Locke's question that Mirabeau was answering; and Mirabeau was, for a time at least, the voice of History. Both question and answer were, for the rest, unambiguous. The latter, reduced to its very simplest terms by a recent writer, runs as follows: "Nous, l'immense majorité,

[16]*Constitution de l'an III*, "Déclaration des droits et des devoirs de l'homme et du citoyen," Art. 6.
[17]Comte Emmanuel Joseph Sieyès, *Qu'est-ce que le tiers état?* (Paris: A Coreard, 1822), p. 197 (italics mine).
[18]Honoré Gabriel Riquetti Mirabeau, *Œuvres* (Paris: Lecointe et Pougin, 1834), I, p. 169 (italics mine). The lines here reproduced are from a speech delivered on July 29th, 1789.

nous avons le droit de faire la loi à vous, l'infime minorité."[19] But a re-
joinder came thundering from across the Channel:

Are we to deny to a *majority* of the people the right of altering even the whole
frame of their society, if such should be their pleasure? They [the revolutionists
in France] may change it, say they, from a monarchy to a republic today, and tomorrow back again from a republic to a monarchy. . . . They are masters of the
commonwealth. . . . The French Revolution, say they, was the act of the majority of the people; and if the majority of any other people, the people of England,
for instance, wish to make the same change, they have the same right.
  Just the same undoubtedly. That is, none at all.[20]

Burke had grasped the true meaning of the things being said in Paris,
the latter never having been put forward as relevant merely to the French
situation. He became anxious, as many others have done since, when they
have contemplated the possibility of majority-rule at home; and his
anxiety is written upon many of the pages of his *Appeal from the New to
the Old Whigs*, and his *Reflections on the French Revolution.*[21] Along
with the anxiety there is much wisdom about Locke's (*i.e.*, Mirabeau's)
question, and the answer which Locke and Mirabeau (and *possibly* Rousseau) had given—wisdom of which the majority-rule democrats have not
yet taken sufficient notice.

"Cette maxime est incontestable." "No right at all." So the issue
was joined; and, as it divided Burke not only from the revolutionary
leaders in France but also from those (*e.g.*, Fox) whom he suspected of
sympathy with them, so it has divided men ever since. There is a sense
in which it is the central problem both of modern politics and of modern
political theory, a sense in which a complete bibliography of the problem
would include almost everything that has been written about politics since
1789. There is a sense in which even those who most deliberately avoid
it can be said, not unfairly, to have written to it, committing themselves,
as they proceed, to positions which stamp them either as friendly or as
unfriendly to the claims of popular majorities to power in the state. There
is a sense in which every shift in power-relations in any state must be
interpreted as a victory or as a defeat for the majority-rule democrats.

There is another sense in which (borrowing a phrase from the contemporary literature of county government) the debate about majority-
rule is the "dark continent" of modern political theory. Theorists have,
on the whole, preferred to attack the problem of majority-rule at its
periphery rather than at its center; and the historians of political theory,
in interpreting (for those who must read as they run) the political ideas
of our forbears, have ordinarily felt little or no responsibility for making
clear the implications of their thought with regard to the ultimate choice

---

[19]Nicolas Saripolos, *La démocratie et l'élection proportionnelle* (Paris: Arthur Rousseau
1899), p. 220 (italics mine).
[20]Burke, *op. cit.*, p. 76 (italics mine in final paragraph).
[21]Edmund Burke, *Reflections on the French Revolution* (London: J. M. Dent & Sons, Ltd.,
1910).

between majority- and minority-rule. For this there are several reasons: In the first place, since 1789 (or thereabouts) political theorists have been increasingly skeptical regarding the possibility of separating, even for purposes of discussion, the "political" from the "economic"—and, latterly, regarding the utility of maintaining any distinction between them at all. This has entailed, for one thing, a growing concern on the part of students of politics with problems of economic theory and organization and with (*e.g.*) the debate regarding the respective merits of capitalism and socialism—a responsibility which they could discharge only at the price of neglecting what less enlightened ages had regarded as primarily political problems. Life being short and theory long, there are sharp upper limits to the time a man can give to the problem of *how* social decisions ought to be made when a considerable part of his time is mortgaged to investigation of the problem (certainly an important one) of what shape these decisions ought to take. It has entailed, for another thing, the injection into the concept of democracy[22] and the concept of majority-rule[23] (assuming for the moment the validity of the distinction sometimes drawn between them) of an *economic* content; with the result that democracy is identified now with capitalism and now with socialism, and men unhesitatingly take it for granted that majority-rule is merely another expression for the economic emancipation of the poor.[24] How far this blurring of concepts has now gone may be seen, on the one hand, in the writings of Everett Dean Martin, who since he is unable to conceive of democracy outside a capitalist context would be hard put to it to salvage the distinction between capitalism and democracy, and, on the other hand, in the writings of Harold J. Laski and Max Lerner. At the limit, the thought of these latter writers expresses itself in such politico-economic amalgams as "democratic collectivism"[25] and "economic democracy"[26]—*i.e.*, the confusion of categories becomes a complete interpenetration.[27] And the result, with respect to the clarity of our outlook

[22]Cf. Everett Dean Martin, "The Place of Government in Modern Economic Society," *Annals of the American Academy of Political and Social Science,* CCVI (November, 1939), p. 14: "This is the very essence of democratic liberal government—the consent of the governed. Even on the assumption that there is a scientific technology adequate to control the entire economic life of a nation, ... it is clear that governmental planning is incompatible with the consent of the governed."

[23]Cf. Max Lerner, *It Is Later Than You Think* (New York: Viking Press, 1938), p. 97: "There can be no significant or lasting political democracy that is not based upon economic democracy. . . . It is like having a handsome and impressive architectural façade when behind it the walls are loose and the plaster crumbling." Mr. Lerner does *not* distinguish between democracy and majority-rule. Cf. *ibid.,* p. 98: "Democracy . . . . means the rule of the majority through a set of representatives chosen by direct election."

[24]Cf. Harold J. Laski, *Democracy in Crisis* (London: George Allen & Unwin, Ltd., 1934), p. 233: "The logic of universal suffrage is either an equal society or such a continuous expansion of material welfare as softens the contrast between rich and poor."

[25]Lerner, *op. cit.,* p. 159.

[26]Harold J. Laski, *Parliamentary Government in England* (New York: Viking Press, 1938), p. 69: "A political democracy seeks, by its own inner impulses, to become a social and *economic democracy*" (italics mine).

[27]Cf. R. M. MacIver, *Leviathan and the People* (Baton Rouge: Louisiana State University Press, 1939), p. 162: "Democracy is a type of *political* structure. It premises the equality of men *as citizens,* with respect therefore to their rights as voters and their rights before the law. The question at issue is whether their political equality involves, logically or psychologically, social and economic equality as well. On neither ground is the identification justified."

upon recent historical phenomena, may be assessed when we raise such a question as the following: Given a "people" of whom (say) sixty per cent are committed to the perpetuation of a capitalist economic system, and forty per cent to its replacement by a socialist economic system, what is the "democratic" solution? Such a question, in the light of recent (post-war) tendencies in Germany, England, France, Spain, *etc.*, can hardly be called unrealistic; and if Professor Laski and Professor Lerner were to give the reply to which they appear to stand committed by their recent pronouncements, or, reversing the proportions, Professor Martin the reply to which he appears to stand committed by his, then the time has indeed come either to abandon the formal separation between economics and political science or to straighten out our thinking with respect to the division of field between them. Meanwhile, the leading economic theorists of our day (Pigou, Keynes, Taussig, Knight, *et al.*) cannot be accused of having questioned the validity and usefulness of the separation; and any attempt to fuse the two disciplines would have to reckon with relentless opposition from that quarter.[28] What the choice ought to be is a matter which lies far beyond the proper scope of the present study; but the fact that there is a choice to be made provides a partial explanation of the avoidance, by recent political theory, of the central issue between majority- and minority-rule. For sober discussion of majority-rule (whether friendly or unfriendly) necessarily abstracts from the content of decisions and fixes attention upon the method of making them. It is a problem which becomes meaningless outside the context of a sharp separation between the subject matter of economic science and that of political science.

A second barrier to direct treatment of the problem of majority-rule in the political theory of the recent past has been what we may fairly call the quest for historical "inevitabilities"—a quest which, at the limit, rests upon premises which reduce the issue at stake between the defenders and opponents of majority-rule to mere triviality. If, for example, the course of history is always determined by *some* minority, or if the majority always gets its way as a matter of course, or if politics is necessarily the pale reflection of an economic reality which is itself determined by immutable laws of history, there would appear to be no more point in canvassing the respective merits of majority- and minority-rule than in canvassing the respective merits of (*e.g.*) cold and warm weather; and to an astonishing extent recent political theory has concerned itself (as, in order to deal with such giants as Hegel, Marx, and Spengler, it appar-

---

[28]Note, for example, how neatly it is maintained in the following statement from a contemporary economist: "Either it [the majority of the population] is permitted to express its collective will or it is suppressed by a dominant minority or its position is somewhere between these extremes. The extent to which it may express its will is a measure of the degree of democracy prevailing" (William L. Hopkins, "The Framework for the Use of Labor," *Annals of the American Academy of Political and Social Science*, CCVI [November, 1939], p. 42). Pro-

ently must) with problems of precisely this nature.[29] We do not raise here the question whether the shift of interest in this direction has been wise or justifiable, our point being merely that it has involved as a logical necessity neglect of and disparagement for the problem dealt with in these pages. This does not mean, of course, that in order to hold an opinion about majority-rule one must repudiate the notion of social law and embrace Dr. Johnson's doctrine that the will is free and there's an end to it; but it is undoubtedly true that the reality and importance which a given theorist is likely to concede to the question posed by the majority-rule democrats depend upon the degree of indeterminacy which he attributes to political events. No indeterminacy, no problem.

A third development which has done much to prevent political theorists from making the debate about majority-rule one of their central pre-occupations has been the growing incidence of the belief that the choice between majority-rule and minority-rule is a false dilemma. We have already noticed, in speaking of Plato, an early expression of that belief— i.e., Plato's argument that the excellent judge is neither he who gives the

fessor Laski and Professor Lerner, on the other hand, appear to be saying that in the absence of a considerable measure of economic equality the extent to which the majority of the population is able to effectuate its will is *not* a reliable index of the "degree of democracy prevailing" —whatever may be the case where the requisite measure of economic equality is present. Now: since the societies with which we are familiar are societies from which the requisite measure of economic equality is clearly absent, they can hardly avoid the conclusion that in attempting to classify these societies, we dare not accept the existence of facilities for the expression (and, as Professor Hopkins would presumably add, the implementation) of the will of the majority as evidence of democratic character. And, while it seems improbable that either of the writers referred to would, if faced directly with this question, take the position that such facilities are valueless, from the democratic point of view, in a (for them) inappropriate economic context, the insistence upon economic equality as an indispensable precondition for democracy can, as with Lenin, easily conduce to such a position. The danger, as Sidney Hook has ably shown ("Reflections on the Russian Revolution," *Southern Review*, IV [1939], p. 461), is that one will end up by claiming democratic sanctions for the decrees of an *authoritarian* government on the grounds that it is promoting economic equality; and no one is really safe from that danger, in the present writer's opinion, until he has freed himself from the temptation to call undemocratic those societies with whose economic policies he does not happen to sympathize. To assign a specific economic content to the concept of majority-rule democracy is, in effect, to question the majority's crucial right to exercise its own judgment in shaping the outlines of its economic system.

It is not necessary, in order to press this point, to look forward less eagerly than Professor Laski and Professor Lerner, or, for that matter, than Lenin, to the time when existing "democracies" shall have learned to operate their economic systems at full capacity, and to distribute the product in such a fashion as to abolish poverty. Nor is it necessary to repudiate their conviction that the extremes of poverty with which we are today familiar prevent large numbers of men from making the most of the political rights which they enjoy under existing "democratic" constitutions. Nor, finally, is it necessary to wish less fervently than they that those who are so prevented shall soon be admitted to a fuller share of the good things which a smoothly-functioning economic system might provide. But much confusion could be avoided if those who see eye to eye on these issues were to adopt the simple expedient of calling a society which denies this fuller share to some of its members a "bad" (*i.e.*, not *the* "good") society, reserving the term "undemocratic" for those societies in which decision-making power has become concentrated in the hands of a numerical minority. This would, to be sure, involve the admission (which the writers in question are apparently reluctant to make) that a society can acquire the paraphernalia of democracy without thereby becoming the good society, but it would greatly facilitate the task of defining those paraphernalia. The most that the social sciences can hope finally to offer to activists is (a) a theoretically defensible blue-print of a "good" political system, (b) a theoretically defensible blue-print of a "good" economic system, and (c) a clear picture of the social changes we must effectuate in order to translate each into reality. The question whether a good economic system can exist in the absence of a good political system, or a good political system in the absence of a good economic system (the latter being the question to which Professor Lerner and Professor Laski are really addressing themselves) is obviously posterior to the task of defining these things; and it is of this methodological consideration that the political scientists (but not the economists) have lately been unmindful.

[29]The concept of an absolute historical determinism, corresponding in its way to the political *heimarmenē* of the later Stoics, seems to be, for reasons which cannot be clearly determined, much in the air in the contemporary world. Thus we find the doctrine developed not only in the vast and overwhelming work of Spengler, but in the thought of many lesser writers. Among

majority ascendancy over the minority nor he who gives the minority ascendancy over the majority, but rather that one who gives them both *laws* in the observance of which they may live together as friends. The notion reappears in the *Politics* of Aristotle, who, though not unconscious of the difficulties involved in putting it into practice, nevertheless treated it as an objective whose realization lay within the bounds of the possible.[30] It was, again, an important element in the "natural law" doctrines of the Middle Ages, the essence of which was an insistence that good law is a "given" which, wholly independent of human volition, is to be "discovered" either by the exercise of reason or the consultation of books and documents which "reveal" the will of God. It recurs in Harrington's dream of a "government of laws and not of men,"[31] in Rousseau's "volonté générale" (which both was and was not independent of human volition), and finally, in modern "constitutionalism"—*i.e.*, in all the attempts which men have made to bind themselves and their descendants to rules whose reasonableness has seemed, at the moment of their enactment, beyond challenge. The theory holds that men subsequently obey such rules not because they are the will of the majority or the will of the minority, but because they are the Law; and, while it is a conception which readily lends itself to caricature[32] (as also to exploitation!), such has been its appeal to minds which have commanded universal respect that we should, perhaps, apply to it the rule which Sir Joshua Reynolds is said to have applied to Livy and Raphael and Michelangelo:

If ever we should find ourselves disposed not to admire [it, we should] . . . . not . . . . follow our own fancies, but . . . . study . . . . until we know how and what

works notable for their diversity of accent and argumentation as well as the general similarity of their theses we may cite: C. H. Von Méray, *Weltmutation* (Zürich: Max Rascher, 1918); F. Vipper, *Krugovorot istorii* (of which a précis appears in the *Revue historique*, CLXIII [1930], pp. 160 ff.); Karl Joël, *Wandlungen der Weltanschauung* (Tübingen: Propyläen Verlag, 2 vols., 1928-1934); Alexander Raven, *Civilization as Divine Superman* (London: Williams & Norgate, 1932); Eugenio d'Ors (whose theories are developed in a series of articles on "Métahistoire" in the *Revue des questions historiques* in 1934-1936); Pitirim A. Sorokin, *Social and Cultural Dynamics* (New York: Macmillan Co., 3 vols., 1936-1938); Arnold J. Toynbee, *A Study of History* (London: Oxford Press, 6 vols., 1934-1939). It is, of course, possible to use the prevalence of the theory as argument for its validity, as does Spengler in his *Decline of the West* (translated by Charles F. Atkinson, New York: Alfred A. Knopf, 2 vols., 1928), I, p. xv: "I am convinced that it is not merely a question of writing one out of several possible and merely logically justifiable philosophies, but of writing *the* philosophy of our time, one that is to some extent a natural philosophy and is dimly presaged by all. . . . [It is] an idea that is historically essential—that does not occur within an epoch but itself makes that epoch. . . . It belongs to our time as a whole and influences all thinkers, without their knowing it." Cf. *ibid.*, pp. 159-160, where the doctrine of determinism is said to be "the *last* great task of Western philosophy, the only one which still remains in store for the aged wisdom of the Faustian Culture. . . . The physiognomic of world-happening will become the *last Faustian philosophy.*" Cf. Lawrence Dennis, *The Dynamics of War and Revolution* (New York: The Weekly Foreign Letter, 1940), pp. xx-xxi: "It has always seemed to me that, in any objective sense of the term, all governments and societies everywhere in the world today, above the level of the tribal stage of culture, have to be democratic. That is to say, they must be governments more or less of the people, by the people and for the people. . . . The more arbitrarily and violently a people are governed today, the more dependent their government must be on continuous sanction by the will of a substantial majority. Otherwise, such a government would be overthrown overnight by an almost [!] spontaneous revolt of the dissatisfied majority."

[30] Aristotle, *op. cit.*, iii. 11. 1282b: "Laws, when good, should be supreme. . . . The magistrate or magistrates should regulate those matters only on which the laws are unable to speak with precision *owing to the difficulty of any general principle embracing all particulars*" (italics mine). Cf. *ibid.*, i. 5. 1254a: "That some should rule and others be ruled is a thing not only necessary, but expedient."

[31] James Harrington, *Oceana* (Heidelberg: C. Winter, 1924).

[32] As in Morris Cohen's phrase, "communal ghosts in political theory." Cf. Morris R. Cohen, *Reason and Nature* (New York: Harcourt Brace & Co., 1931), p. 386.

we ought to admire; and if we cannot arrive at the combination of admiration with knowledge, rather . . . . believe that we are dull, than that the rest of the world has been imposed on.[33]

That is, we should do, with respect to this theory, that which, according to the presuppositions of constitutionalism, majorities ought to do *vis-à-vis* constitutional rules which do not commend themselves to their approval. Without, however, calling into question the validity of the theory, it can be observed that the gulf fixed between those who can and those who cannot make sense of the notion of a "government of laws and not of men" is a very wide one, and that the debate about majority-rule is likely to seem much more urgent to those who cannot see any sense in it (and thus see minority-rule as the only other possibility) than to those who can. It can be observed, further, that the former find themselves obliged to conceive the problem in the following terms: The situation with regard to any particular rule at any particular moment is: (a) all are in favor of it, or (b) all are opposed to it, or (c) some are in favor of it and some are opposed to it. If (a), the rule will be observed as a matter of course. If (b), the rule will not be observed because no one will so much as raise the question. If (c), the opponents of the rule are (save in case of a tie) either more numerous or less numerous than its supporters; and since one of the two groups must now subject itself to a rule which it opposes, the fact that the other group is getting its way[34] cannot be covered over by a euphemism regarding government by laws.[35] This is not, by any means, to disregard the possibility envisaged by Professor MacIver, who points out that the majority may acquiesce because it belongs to a larger majority which demands that the entire body of laws not be placed at the mercy of any bare majority which seeks to change them.[36] This is undoubtedly a familiar phenomenon in modern politics. But the bare majority which wills a change and cannot secure it becomes, in this regard, subject to the will of the opposing minority; and nothing is really gained by representing it as subject to law rather than to the will of that minority.

A fourth consideration to which we may point in explaining the neglect of the problem of majority-rule in recent political theory is what

---

[33]Burke, "An Appeal from the New to the Old Whigs," p. 114.

[34]Cf. J. C. L. Simonde de-Sismondi, *Études sur les constitutions des peuples libres* (Paris: Treuttel et Würtz, 1836), p. 144: "Chacun n'est libre, et à plus forte raison souverain, qu'autant que sa propre volonté s'accorde avec la volonté dominante; mais celui qui soumet sa volonté à une volonté contraire à la sienne n'est qu'un sujet."

[35]Cf. T. E. Holland, *The Elements of Jurisprudence* (Oxford: The Clarendon Press, 1924), p. 46, where a state is defined as a "numerous assemblage of human beings, generally occupying a certain territory, amongst whom *the will of the majority, or of an ascertainable class of persons,* is by the strength of such a majority, or class, made to prevail against any of their number who oppose it" (italics mine). Note that Holland considers no third possibility, and thus aligns himself with the position set forth in the text. Cf. Joseph Story, *Commentaries on the Constitution* (Boston: Little Brown & Co., 2 vols., 1858), I, p. 269: "There could be but one of two rules adopted in all governments, either, that the majority should govern, or the minority should govern."

[36]MacIver, *op. cit.*, p. 152: "It is the larger majority for the broader issue limiting the right of any small emergent majority within it lest by action directed solely to particular issues it defeat the greater consensus. *The proviso is obviously exposed to the risk that it confers a veto power on a mere minority,* but it is at least susceptible of a different construction. It is an approach to what Rousseau considered the 'general will' " (italics mine).

we may call the tendency to write off the idea of majority-decisions as a matter which does not lend itself to theoretical treatment.[37] "La loi de la majorité," wrote M. Esmein, "est une de ces idées simples qui se font accepter d'emblée."[38] It is, that is to say, like the axioms of Euclidean geometry; you look at it and you *know* it to be true.[39] To attempt to demonstrate it would, therefore, be like trying to demonstrate the law of contradiction itself. And, while no other writer of distinction appears to have made such a claim for it in so many words,[40] agreement with M. Esmein is perhaps the most charitable hypothesis upon which we may explain the behavior of the many writers who, without attempting to demonstrate its validity, have proclaimed their allegiance to the principle and hurried on to other matters[41]—or assumed its validity in the course of a discussion of some other problem.[42] Ranged against M. Esmein, on the other hand, are a numerous body of writers who have been inclined to dismiss the majority-principle as a notion too preposterous to be worthy of serious attention—*i.e.*, as a notion whose *invalidity* is self-evident.[43] The chuckle in the following lines from Jellinek does not, for example, conceal either their high seriousness or the supposed axiomatic character of their inarticulate premise:

Dass zwei von vornherein mehr werth sein sollten als einer, widersprach den kraftvollen Individualitätsgefühl, das namentlich die germanischen Völker auszeichnete. Wenn ein kühner Mann in offenen Kampfe fünf überwinden konnte, warum sollte er sich im Rathe der Mehrheit beugen?[44]

---

[37]Cf. Georg Jellinek, *Das Recht der Minoritäten* (Wien: Alfred Hölder, 1898), p. 1: "Dass Mehrheit den Ausschlag gebe dort, wo es gilt Beschlüsse zu fassen, sei es bei Wahlen, sei es in der Gesetzgebung oder in verwaltenden und richtenden Collegien, erscheint uns heute so selbstverständlich, dass wir auf eine nähere Begründung verzichten zu müssen glauben." He adds, however (*ibid.*): "Und dennoch ist der Satz, dass Mehrheit entscheide, nichts weniger als selbstverständlich." Cf. Gierke, *op. cit.*, p. 565: "Infolge solcher allgemeinen Annerkennung nehmen wir heute das Majoritätsprinzip als etwas Selbstverständliches hin und zerbrechen uns nicht viel den Kopf darüber, warum denn hier überall der Teil so viel gilt wie das Ganze. Auch in juristischen, politischen, und philosophischen Schriften begegnen nur selten, eingehender Versuche seiner Rechtfertigung."

[38]A. Esmein, *Éléments de droit constitutionnel français et comparé* (Paris: Librairie J. B. Sirey, 1906), p. 225.

[39]Cf. Marie Collins Swabey, *Theory of the Democratic State* (Cambridge: Harvard University Press, 1937), p. 26: "It is as much an axiom of quantity that what there is more of should be accounted more as that equals should be accounted equal." All would agree; but some would ask, How much more?

[40]Cf. Willmoore Kendall, "The Majority Principle and the Scientific Elite," *Southern Review*, IV (1939), p. 475: "Precisely the most interesting fact about the majority principle . . . . is that some minds regard it as *obviously true*, and others regard it as *obviously false*. This is important because . . . . we waste our time when we seek the grounds upon which a man will defend a proposition which he treats as self-evident. . . . The most you can hope to do . . . . is to compile a history of how he came to believe [it]." Cf. Swabey, *op. cit.*, p. 11: "Democracy, as is well known, stakes its case on the inherent reasonableness (once called the 'self-evidence') of its ideas."

[41]*E.g.*, Floyd Henry Allport, *Institutional Behavior* (Chapel Hill: University of North Carolina Press, 1933), p. 81: "The only way out of this muddle, in my opinion, is to stop talking about the feasibility of a certain scheme for running the country and find out what we who are citizens, or what a substantial majority of us, want. What justification have we for abandoning the conviction that individuals are competent judges of their own needs?" Cf. J. W. Studebaker, *Plain Talk* (Washington: National Home Library Association, 1936), p. 147: "I am willing to wait for solutions until the majority is intelligent enough to support them."

[42]Such, *e.g.*, was the invariable procedure of J. Allen Smith, the most uncompromising of recent majority-rule democrats in the United States. See his *The Spirit of American Government* (New York: Macmillan Co., 1912), *passim*. See also Albert M. Kales, *Unpopular Government in the United States* (Chicago: University of Chicago Press, 1914), *passim*.

[43]An interesting compromise between these two positions is that put forward by Ruffini Avondo (*op. cit.*, p. 7): "Il principio maggioritario è naturale [in the preceding sentence he has coupled *naturale* with *intuitivo*] in questo solo senso, e cioè fino a tanto che lo si contrappone al suo assurdo e non mai esistito inverso, il principio minoritario."

[44]Jellinek, *op. cit.*, p. 2.

Similarly, Anatole France's quip to the effect that "foolishness repeated by thirty million mouths is none the less foolishness,"[45] suggesting as it does the reply that a tautology by Anatole France is still a tautology, is in effect a denial that the majority-principle can be supported by rational arguments; and a like emphasis may be detected in Brooks Adams' *bon mot* to an acquaintance who had remarked that Mr. Adams did not appear to think very highly of democracy: "Do you think I'm a damned fool?"[46] Equally in point here are the commentaries of contemporary critics upon theorists who have attempted to defend the principle: Professor Sabine, for example, classifies Locke's belief in the "inevitable wisdom of majority decisions" as one of his "more doubtful ideas"[47] with a casualness which philosophical critics might well reserve for such matters as Bishop Berkeley's faith in the therapeutic properties of barley-water. Professor Catlin, who chides Rousseau for having "brusqued" the question "why the *majority* will alone—that of the numerical majority—should be the index of the General Will,"[48] observes in reply that neither Aristotle nor Montesquieu believed any such thing,[49] and apparently supposes that no further refutation of the notion is needed. Carritt can speak drolly of the "divine right of majorities" in the same breath with the "divine right of kings,"[50] thus disposing—with an adjective—of those who feel that there is at least *something* more to be said for the right of majorities than for the right of kings; and, in the same book, he permits himself to write off as a "weakness" *tout court* Locke's "argument that majority-rule is somehow specially consonant with the law of reason."[51] And Professors Sabine and Shepard succeed in composing a ninety-page introduction to Krabbe's *The Modern Idea of the State*,[52] the most vigorous of recent philosophical defenses of majority-rule, without even taking notice of this aspect of its argument—much as a charitable critic of Mill might, in writing about him, overlook the fact that he opposed government interference with the traffic in narcotic drugs!

In the light of the foregoing considerations, it is not altogether surprising that the bibliography appended to the article on Majority Rule in the *Encyclopaedia of the Social Sciences* includes hardly more than a dozen items. Less easy to explain, however, are the preponderance in that bibliography of Polish (Konopczyński, Starosolskyj, Stawski) and

[45]Anatole France, *ap.* Catlin, *The Science and Method of Politics* (London: Kegan Paul, Trench, Trubner & Co., 1927), pp. 348-349.
[46]Brooks Adams, *ap.* R. P. Blackmur, "Henry and Brooks Adams," *Southern Review*, V (1939), p. 316.
[47]George H. Sabine, *A History of Political Theory* (New York: Henry Holt & Co., 1937), p. 540.
[48]Catlin, *Story of the Political Philosophers*, p. 453.
[49]*Ibid.*, p. 454.
[50]E. A. Carritt, *Morals and Politics* (Oxford: Oxford University Press, 1935), p. 7. The writer has been unable to find any defenders of the majority-principle who claim divine sanctions for it. Cf. Starosolskyj, *op. cit.*, p. 39.
[51]*Ibid.*, p. 78.
[52]Hugo Krabbe, *The Modern Idea of the State*, translated by George H. Sabine and Walter J. Shepard (New York: D. Appleton & Co., 1922), "Translators' Introduction," pp. xi-lxxxi.

German (Gierke, Simmel) names, the absence of a single book-length study on the subject by an English or an American writer, and, on another level (since the compilers of the bibliography can hardly be blamed if Poles and Germans do, and Englishmen and Americans do not, write on majority-rule), the exclusion of such obviously relevant items as Locke's *Second Treatise,* Rousseau's *Du contrat social*[53] and *Considérations sur le gouvernement de Pologne,*[54] Burke's *Reflections on the French Revolution* and *Appeal from the New to the Old Whigs,* and all the more recent masterpieces of democratic theory. While, as we have already intimated, by no means all are agreed that democracy and majority-rule are the same thing, the democratic movement has for a long while had within its ranks politicians and theorists who have sought to *make* them the same thing— *i.e.,* to *change* democracy in the direction of majority-rule; and those who have stepped forward to defend the "constitutionalist" and minority-rights aspect of democracy have consequently found themselves obliged to become participants in what we may properly call the "debate" about majority-rule. The theory of the democratic state is, therefore, to a large extent devoted to a discussion which is germane to Konopczyński's problem; and, whatever one's opinion may be as to the proper relation between democracy and majority-rule, students of the latter have at their disposal a vast body of literature (much of which *is* in English) to which —as anyone may see from a glance at Starosolskyj's and Stawski's footnotes—they have not given the attention it deserves. And no writer at the present time can afford to neglect such works as Krabbe's *Die moderne Staats-idee*[55] and C. J. Friedrich's *Constitutional Government and Politics,*[56] distinguished contemporary contributions to the problem, though neither puts itself forward as a work on majority-rule.

How did the compilers of the bibliography in the *Encyclopedia* happen to overlook the representative works in democratic theory (and anti-democratic theory, for the critics of democracy have often been no less eager than the majority-rule democrats to insist upon the identity between democracy and majority-rule[57])? The explanation is, in the opinion of the present writer, to be sought in the fact that, although the expressions "majority-rule," "principle of majority-rule," "majority principle," *etc.,* have for a long while been familiar to students of politics and sociology, no attempt has been made to define them with scientific precision—with the result that, to this day, we are without any unambiguous terminological distinction between (a) the *rule* by which (explicitly, as

[53]J. J. Rousseau, *Œuvres complètes* (Paris: P. Dupont, 1823), V, pp. 61-242.
[54]*Ibid.,* pp. 243-385.
[55]H. Krabbe, *Die moderne Staats-idee* (Haag: Martinus Nijhoff, 1919).
[56]Carl Joachim Friedrich, *Constitutional Government and Politics* (New York: Harper and Brothers, 1937). It should be noticed that this volume appeared after the publication of Konopczyński's article and the bibliography annexed to it.
[57]Cf. Ruffini Avondo, *op. cit.,* p. 113: "[I] publicisti avversi alla democrazia . . . . tendono per lo più ad accollare al principio maggioritario la responsabilità di tutti i mali attribuiti alle instituzioni democratiche."

with the Dutch chamber, or by tacit understanding, as with the American Senate and the American House of Representatives) organized bodies are committed to decisions by majority-vote, (b) the *theory* according to which political power should be vested in the numerical majority of the "people," and (c) the form of government which the defenders of (b) would like to see adopted wherever it does not yet exist, and continued wherever it does exist. Of the three, (b) and (c) are apparently the most intimately related, since (c) is the state of affairs which (b) enjoins and (b) is the theory which enjoins that state of affairs—since, again, the explicit reference of both is to *politics, i.e.,* to the state. It is quite otherwise with (a) since—although (c) is the form of government which results when a *people* adopts (a) as a rule for making decisions, and (b) is a theory which urges that peoples adopt such a rule—(a) is constantly employed in all manner of "groups" which have nothing to do with politics in the ordinary sense of the word, *e.g.,* Boy Scout troops, churches, scientific organizations, business corporations, *etc.* It is, of course, true that to the extent that there is a "government" at all in a Boy Scout troop which has adopted (a), it becomes (in a manner of speaking) an illustration of (c), as, also, that those members of the troop who would, on principle, resist a move to delegate decision-making authority to the Senior Patrol Leader are (in a manner of speaking) exponents of (b).[58] It is true, too, that an adequate account of (c), or an adequate exposition of (b), would need to take account of whatever the sociologists have to say about (a), as, also, that a complete account of (a) in a sociological treatise would have to take account of what the political scientists have to say about (c) and the political theorists about (b). But, at the limit, (a), (b), and (c) are, as we have stated them, clearly distinguishable from one another, just as, in economics, the principle of competition, the doctrine of laissez-faire, and the competitive system may be distinguished from one another for purposes of discussion. It is, therefore, regrettable that the same term, the "majority principle," has for a long while had to do service for both (b) and (a)—the word "principle" being construed, in the one case, by analogy with (*e.g.*) the "principle of the divine right of kings," and in the other case, by analogy with (*e.g.*) the "principle of primogeniture" (= the legal rule by which an exclusive right of inheritance is assigned to first-born children) ; and that the term "majority-rule" may denote either (a) or (c) according as we understand "rule" to mean "government" (by analogy with minority-rule) or "law" (by analogy with "rule

---

[58]Thus such a book as *The Modern Corporation and Private Property,* by A. A. Berle and Gardiner C. Means, (New York: The Macmillan Co., 1934), insofar as it is a plea for the transfer of power in the modern corporation from unresponsible directorates to the shareholders (acting by majority vote on a one-share, one-vote basis), is, in that sphere, a defense of what we are about to define as the doctrine of majority-rule. Whether or not Mr. Berle would favor the transfer of power to make decisions about foreign policy from an unresponsible Department of State to the electorate (acting by majority-vote on any basis) the writer has been unable to learn; but if the argument of the following paragraphs of the text be correct, it would be unwise to make inferences regarding his opinion on the second question from his opinion on the first.

of closure") ; and that "principle of majority rule" (or "principle of majority-rule") is used interchangeably with "majority principle" to denote either (a) or (b).[59] Usually, of course, when we come across one of these expressions we can easily decide which of its possible meanings is intended by reference to the context in which it appears. When Professor Carpenter tells us that "the principle of majority rule is therefore a device which, although it contains no inherent ethical validity, affords a practical means whereby groups of people may reach decisions,"[60] we may be fairly certain that he is speaking of (a)—although, since it is difficult to conceive of a *device* which possesses "inherent ethical validity," we may at least consider the possibility that he is speaking of (b). When, again, he tells us that "the clearest expression of the majority principle was stated [*sic*] by Frederick Grimke,"[61] and we find the following passage cited as evidence of this fact, we know that he is speaking of (b):

> If, in laying the foundations of government, our design is to consult the common interests of the whole population, there is no alternative but the rule of the majority. If when the vote is taken, either among the citizens at large, or in the legislative body which represents them, the will of the greater number did not prevail, the minority would be at liberty to act without rule, not merely as regards themselves, but in regard to the majority also.[62]

When, finally, he tells us that "the evils of majority-rule can never be cured by turning the control of the government over to the minority,"[63] we know that he means by "majority-rule" a state of affairs, *i.e.*, our (c). But it is not always so; and Konopczyński's article is an excellent illustration of the way in which an inadequate division of labor between terms can become a positive hindrance both to clear thinking and to fruitful investigation. "Majority rule," he explains, "thus came to be not only a system prevalent in a certain country [= our (c)?] or an institution or a method of voting [= our (a)?] but, except in a few quarters, an absolute and generally accepted concept.[64] The idea that as a rule truth, reason and justice are on the side of the majority [= our (b)?] became the keystone of the democratic credo."[65] He is, therefore, not wholly unaware of the distinction we have drawn between the rule which provides that the majority is to make the decisions, the theory or belief that the majority ought to make the decisions, and the form of government which results where the rule of decisions by majority-vote is adopted by a state. Since, however, it seems natural to him to employ the same term

---

[59] Cf. J. G. Heinberg, *op. cit.*, p. 452: "The term 'majority rule' is as impossible to escape as it is apparently difficult to define with precision."

[60] W. S. Carpenter, *The Development of American Political Thought* (Princeton: Princeton University Press, 1930), p. 163.

[61] *Ibid.*, p. 162.

[62] Frederick Grimke, *Considerations on the Nature and Tendency of Free Institutions* (New York: Derby & Jackson, 1856), p. 36.

[63] Carpenter, *op. cit.*, p. 163.

[64] Cf. Heinberg, *op. cit.*, p. 457: "The dogma of majority rule [= (b)?] is not a rationalization based upon definite practices but a concept based upon other concepts."

[65] Ladislas Konopczyński, *Encyclopaedia of the Social Sciences* (New York: The Macmillan Co., 1933), X, *s. v.* "Majority Rule." The writer is indebted to Professor Max Lerner for the information that Konopczyński did not prepare the bibliography appended to his article.

to denote all three (as he has certainly done in the passage here reproduced), the moment never comes at which he feels obliged to take *one* of
them as the subject-matter of his essay—with the curious result that his
history of the "keystone of the democratic credo" must finally compete
for space with an account of the social and economic factors governing
the speed with which the device of majority-voting develops, and a discussion of procedural rules in legislative assemblies! Thus, though he
has mentioned (b) in the body of his article, and paid his respects to
(*e.g.*) Locke and Rousseau, (b) receives no attention at all in the bibliography, which concerns itself exclusively with (a)—*i.e.*, with books and
articles by scholars whose bibliographies in turn concern themselves, in
the main, with (a).[66]

Now, obviously, we cannot have at our disposal too much information
about so important a factor in the associational life of the Western world
as the rule according to which (in the phrase we have quoted from
Gierke) "der Teil so viel gilt wie das Ganze," since, as Gierke facetiously
points out, the only differences of opinion to which men have not yet
sought to apply it are those between husband and wife:

Erst unterhalb der Dreizahl versagt dieses Allheilmittel für Meinungsverschieden-
heiten. In der Gemeinschaft zu Zweien gibt es keine Majorität. Die innigste aller
menschlichen Verbindungen, die Ehe, muss sich ohne Abstimmungen behelfen.[67]

It would be interesting to know where the rule originated, what shape it
has taken in various types of social organization and at various stages in
the history of humankind, what (if any) characteristics are common to
the groups which have made use of it, whether groups which do use it
are (*e.g.*) more "efficient," or more long-lived, or more capable of retain-
ing the loyalty of their members, than those which do not, whether (as
some have contended) it is in fact appropriate only to an "advanced"
(*i.e.*, "highly differentiated") stage of social development, *etc.* Gierke's
Das deutsche Genossenschaftsrecht[68] (from which Stawski and Starosolskyj have borrowed most of their data regarding the history of the rule)
is therefore a work for which all students of the social sciences ought to
feel a debt of profound gratitude; and Simmel's "Excursus on the
Majority Principle," in his *Soziologie*[69] is, for the same reason, a discussion which no student of the social sciences can read without subsequently
paying to it the unusual compliment of wishing that it had been many
times as long. It can, nevertheless, hardly be overemphasized that such in-
quiries are, at their best, capable of throwing a very limited amount of
light upon our (b) and (c) when these are conceived with regard solely to

---

[66]Cf. Ruffini Avondo, *op. cit.*, p. 115. "Il principio maggioritario . . . . è semplicemente
una formola giuridica."
[67]Gierke, *op. cit.*, p. 565.
[68]Otto von Gierke, *Das deutsche Genossenschaftsrecht* (Berlin: Weidmann, 4 vols., 1868-
1913).
[69]Georg Simmel, *Soziologie* (Leipzig: Duncker & Humblot, 1908), pp. 186-197.

states, and a still more limited amount of light upon our (b) and (c) when these are conceived with regard solely to states of a certain kind (*i.e.*, "democratic" states). The following considerations should make this abundantly clear even to the most devoted admirers of Gierke and Simmel:

First, while it is undoubtedly true, as Gierke,[70] Stawski,[71] Starosolskyj,[72] and others[73] have argued, that the majority-principle (*qua* rule for making decisions) played an important rôle in some of the constitutions of ancient Greece, and, particularly, in that of Athens, none of the Greek city states ever experimented with what the modern "radical" democrat calls "majority-rule."[74] At Athens, for example, the class of persons who took *no* part in the process by which legislative and judicial decisions were made by majority-vote, was always overwhelmingly larger than that of the active "citizens."[75] This, however, is another way of saying that in its most "democratic" days Athenian government possessed the essential *characteristicum* of those minority-rule situations to which the modern exponents of (b) object.[76] A governing minority does not divest itself of its claim to classification as a government *over* the majority merely by settling differences among its own members by majority-vote—wherefore apologists for "judicial supremacy" in the United States have sagely avoided the argument that the United States Supreme Court is a "democratic" institution because the will of five of its justices always prevails over that of four. And, just as majority-rule in the United States extends, at most, to those matters in which the Supreme Court either affirms the will of the majority (by deciding that a statute is consistent with the language and spirit of the constitution), or adopts a policy of non-intervention (by declaring the question at issue "political"), so majority-rule at Athens must have been confined to those social decisions which were *not* made by majority-vote in the assembly—*i.e.*, precisely where most writers who fail to distinguish between the *loi de la majorité* and what

---

[70]Gierke, "Geschichte des Majoritätsprinzipes," p. 8.
[71]Stawski, *op. cit.*, p. 69.
[72]Starosolskyj, *op. cit.*, p. 5.
[73]Ruffini Avondo, *op. cit.*, pp. 12-13.
[74]*I.e.*, no such régime was ever *established*. It is quite possible, though by no means certain, that what we could identify as majority-rule may have been envisaged by the leaders of—and might, under less adverse circumstances, have resulted from—the two truly radical governments of the ancient world, the one set up at Sparta by Nabis and the Pergamene "demarchy" headed by Aristonicus and a political philosopher and agitator who has been compared to Lenin, Blossius of Cumae. But the history of these movements discloses only revolutionary *dictatorships* which for a little while waged a hopeless struggle against the overwhelming might of foreign armies. For an account of the "liberal" movements of antiquity, see R. von Pöhlmann, *Geschichte der sozialen Frage und des Sozialismus in der antiken Welt* (edited by Friedrich Oertel, München: Beck'sche Verlagbuchhandlung, 1925).
[75]Three large groups excluded from citizenship were metics, slaves, and women. It was taken for granted that all of these had to be excluded from participation in government, although it is supposed that the *Ecclesiazusae* of Aristophanes represents a parodic attack on some serious proposal to enfranchize Athenian women.
[76]But cf. John E. E. Dalberg-Acton, *The History of Freedom and Other Essays* (London: Macmillan & Co., 1907), p. 13: "The lesson of their [Athenian] experience endures for all times, for it teaches that government by the whole, being the government of the most numerous and most powerful class, is an evil of the same nature as unmixed monarchy."

Heinberg amiably calls the "dogma of majority rule,"[77] have been least likely to look for them.

Secondly, the political scientist's estimate of the relevance of data regarding the use of the *loi de la majorité* in churches, business corporations, guilds, *etc.*, to the problem of government by popular majority in the state, must be made with an eye to what Catlin has denominated the distinction between "the voluntary society seeking ultimate ends, values, or goods, and . . . . the coercive society seeking immediate or mundane advantages or goods"—a distinction which Catlin attributes to Francisco Suárez and regards as the "core of political wisdom."[78] The state, whose power the majority-rule democrats would like to see exercised by popular majorities, has always belonged in the past, and seems likely to belong throughout the predictable future, to the second of these two classifications, that of *coercive societies seeking immediate or mundane advantages or goods*; for whatever may be our feeling regarding the Pluralist contention that this thing should not be true,[79] all that we know of the history of mankind suggests the generalization that man's need for an authority which (within a given territory) exacts obedience to its commands is "ultimate" in the same sense as the need for food and shelter. Government by popular majority [= (c) above] is one of the conceivable methods for organizing that authority, as the "dogma of majority-rule" [= (b) above] is one of the theories about the way in which it should be organized, and as the majority-principle [= (a) above] is the rule of which exponents of (b) would have peoples avail themselves where questions arise as to what that authority is to command and subsequently enforce by coercion. Morris Cohen says:

In practice it is often much more important to come to a decision one way or another than to wait for adequate reasons on which to base a right decision. . . .

Political authority . . . . has its basis in . . . . [the] need to have practical controversies settled. When we are parties to a suit, we are anxious that the issue be settled justly, i.e. in our favour[!]. But there is a general interest on the part of all members of the community in having controversies settled one way or another. Otherwise we fall into a state of perpetual war or anarchy.[80]

Either, that is to say, we fight, or we live in anarchy, or we maintain an organization for the making and enforcement of these decisions in which there is an interest on the part of all; and Cohen clearly means that there is that in man, as we encounter him in the world about us and in the history of the past, which makes us sure that he will not tolerate

[77]Heinberg, *op. cit.*, p. 453.
[78]Catlin, *Story of the Political Philosophers*, p. 270. Cf. Bertrand Russell, *Power* (New York: W. W. Norton & Co., 1938), p. 37: "It is the characteristic of civilized communities that direct physical coercion (with some limitations) is the prerogative of the State."
[79]Harold J. Laski, *Authority in the Modern State* (New Haven: Yale University Press, 1919), chap. 1.
[80]Morris Cohen, *op. cit.*, pp. 24-25. Cf. Guicciardini's dictum that expeditious adjudication of disputes between citizens is much more important than just adjudication (Francesco Guicciardini, *Ricordi politici e civili* [edited by Pietro Pancrazi, Firenze: Rinascimento del libro, 1929], 209, 269).

the second of these possibilities, and that he will tolerate the first only as a means to the third. And, precisely because this is true, we must assign, to those who would press analogies between decision-making within the context of *political* authority and decision-making within those contexts where a challenge to authority is by no means necessarily a declaration of war or a bid for anarchy, the burden of proving that such analogies are sound. In the absence of such proof, the political scientist's investigations must be prosecuted on the assumption that the state is sufficiently different from other kinds of social groups to deserve separate study, thus on the assumption that the moment has not come at which sociology should be permitted to absorb political science.[81]

What is here being called in question is the procedure of those writers who, in discussing the majority-principle (*qua* rule) have failed to distinguish (1) between states with limited electorates (*e.g.*, ancient Athens) and states with highly inclusive electorates (*e.g.*, modern England), and (2) between states and other kinds of social groups—or, to put the same thing in another way, the procedure of those writers who, abstracting from the difference between voluntary and coercive groups on the one hand, and that between states with large subject populations and states without large subject populations on the other hand, have treated the *loi de la majorité* as a proper subject for independent study.[82] And our thesis is, for the moment, that once the majority-principle is conceived as operating in a state, and, still more, in a state in which power has been entrusted to the whole people, we have the elements of a problem so patently unique that it *must* be set aside for separate investigation.

In order to avoid terminological confusions of the sort to which attention has been called in an earlier paragraph, we shall, in what follows, adhere strictly to this usage: We shall employ the term "majority-principle" as the English equivalent of *loi de la majorité,* and shall not again use it to denote a theory regarding the proper residence of political power. For the theory according to which state power should be entrusted

---

[81]Cf. Catlin, *Science and Method*, p. 177.

[82]Alone among the writers who have treated the majority-principle (*qua* rule) as a proper subject for investigation, Edoardo Ruffini Avondo (*op. cit.*, pp. 112-113) has recognized a difficulty here: "Non escludo che sia più facile giustificare il diritto di proprietà nel rapporto fra lo scrittore ed il romanzo che sta scrivendo con gli stessi argomenti che lo giustificano nel rapporto fra lo scrittore ed il tavolo su cui scrive, che giutificare [*sic*] il principio maggioritario quando decide fra i più milioni di elettori del presidente degli Stati Uniti d'America con gli stessi argomenti che lo giustificano quando decide fra quei *tres* che bastano a constituire un *collegium.*" Cf. *ibid.*, p. 9: "Ma tutte le storie valgono forse la pena di essere scritte? La storia di un principio così meccanico come quello che regola le manifestazioni collettive di volontà, storia, cioè, di *una pura forma separata dalla sostanza,* che interesse può avere?" (italics mine). He answers, however (*ibid.*): "A questa obbiezione molte risposte si potrebbero dare." Cf. *ibid.*, p. 23, where he points out that the intellectual climate of Christianity creates a special situation with respect to the making of decisions: "Nella funzione di eleggere e di deliberare il Cristianesimo sovrappose alla volontà umana la volontà divina. Ciò introduceva—specialmente nell'elezione—un nuovo fattore ideale e trascendente di tanta potenza, che valse a trasportare l'istituto elettorale dalla sfera del diritto alla sfera della rivelazione." This is well said; and it is noteworthy that the same writer, adopting with respect to the special situation in the church a procedure analogous to that here adopted with respect to states with inclusive electorates, has made it the subject of a separate investigation: Edoardo Ruffini Avondo, "Il principio maggioritario nella storia del diritto canonico," *Archivio giuridico*, XCIII (1925), pp. 15-67.

to popular majorities we shall avail ourselves of the expression "doctrine of majority-rule" which offers (in contrast to "dogma of majority-rule") the not inconsiderable advantage of connoting no *petitio principii* regarding its validity. For the state of affairs which results where the exponents of the doctrine of majority-rule have got their way we shall reserve the term "majority-rule," for the *characteristica* of such a state of affairs "majority-rule procedures," and for its apologists (*i.e.*, the exponents of the doctrine of majority-rule), the expression "majority-rule democrats." Finally, we shall save the terms "majority-rule theory," or "theory of majority-rule," as also their correlate "majority-rule theorists," to denote the search and the searchers for the "principles" or "laws" of majority-rule systems.

It is obvious, in the light of the foregoing discussion, that the faith of the majority-rule democrat involves a good deal more than a belief that decisions regarding the use of coercive power in the state ought to be made in accordance with the majority-principle. For the majority-principle, on this showing, is merely a rule which a *group of given composition* may adopt for the making of decisions. It provides nothing with respect to the qualifications for membership in the group; it provides nothing with respect to the decision-making competence of the group; and it provides nothing with respect to the nature of the questions which are to be submitted for plebiscitary determination by the group's members, or with respect to the machinery for the conduct of polls on such questions as are to be submitted in this manner. It might, as we have already suggested, serve as a rule for making decisions in a state in which the powers of government are exercised by a handful of oligarchs; it might operate in a state which, though extending the right of suffrage to all of its adult citizens, is yet governed in accordance with a constitution which effectively prevents decisions from being made at all except within carefully defined limits (as with the constitution of the United States);[83] it might, finally, be adopted in a state whose inclusive electorate is permitted to pass only upon questions of the most trivial character (the power to make other decisions having been lodged elsewhere)—or in a state in which the electorate is consulted so infrequently (as with the choice of the president in the United States)—or in so clumsy a manner (as with the choice of senators in the United States) as greatly to circumscribe its power to control the course of governmental policy. When, therefore, the majority-rule democrat says (as he is fond of saying)[84] that the majority of the people ought to have their way, he is not merely

[83]Cf. Herman Finer, *Theory and Practice of Modern Government* (London: Methuen and Co., 1932), I, p. 224: "In America Congress is in a perpetual state of nonage, and the people likewise are bound by a testament made by their fathers."
[84]Cf. Smith, *op. cit.*, p. 370: "The will of the majority ought to be the supreme law of the land."

putting in a good word for the majority-principle. He evidently means that, at the limit, one half minus one of the people ought to accommodate themselves to the wishes of one half of the people plus one;[85] but since one half of the people minus one together with one half of the people plus one make up the *whole* people, he may be seen to have committed himself, along with his plea for the employment of the majority-principle as a rule of decision, to the notion of an *inclusive electorate*. Since, again, as any student of modern history knows, there is no way to make sure that one half plus one of the people *will* have their way over one half minus one of the people without (a) conducting polls with a view to discovering what *is* the way of one half of the people plus one, and (b) conducting such polls often enough to lay bare changes in the composition (thus, possibly, in the "way") of the majority as they occur, he may be seen to have committed himself to what we may call the *principle of popular consultation*. And, finally, since the majority of the people cannot have their way as a matter of course where decision-making powers have been permanently withdrawn from the whole people (as when the people of the United States are forbidden to take away from such rotten boroughs as Rhode Island and Nevada their equal representation in the Senate), he may be seen to have committed himself to the *principle of popular sovereignty*.

The majority-rule democrat must, in other words, establish the case for universal and (formally) equal suffrage, the case for (formal) popular sovereignty, and the case for (at least some machinery of) popular consultation, along with the case for decisions by majority-vote. He must establish the case for universal suffrage because in the absence of universal suffrage there exists no reason for supposing that the decision favored by a majority of the voters is favored also by a majority of the people—that for equal suffrage because the rule committing the minority to accept the decision of the majority as the equivalent of a unanimous decision obviously has the effect of placing in the hands of *each* voter the power to cast the deciding vote, thus of making all voters formally equal.[86] He must demonstrate the case for formal popular

---

[85]Cf. Ruffini Avondo, *Il principio maggioritario*, p. 20, where he speaks of the "fatto giuridicamente incontestabile, che, se vale il principio maggioritario, una maggioranza della metà più uno ha diritti eguali a quelli della totalità."

[86]Cf. Ruffini Avondo, *op. cit.*, p. 8: "L'applicazione del sistema maggioritario presuppone, invero, uno dei principî più giusti ma meno naturali: quello che tutti gli uomini siano eguali fra loro." The passage is significant as an illustration of what happens when an investigator, writing in an age preoccupied with *political* problems, sits down to write about the majority-principle as defined above. Cf. *ibid.*, p. 7: "La comunissima regola, per cui in una collettività debba prevalere quello che vogliono i più e non quello che vogliono i meno, racchiude uno dei più singolari problemi che abbiano affaticato la mente umana." He thus means the rule employed, *e.g.*, by the United States Supreme Court, "un principio così meccanico . . . . una pura forma separata dalla sostanza" (*ibid.*, p. 9), the effect of which, however, is merely to make formally equal the members of the particular collectivity in which it is adopted. It is simply not true that the Supreme Court, in handing down a five to four decision, takes for granted the validity of the proposition that "tutti gli uomini siano eguali fra loro." The author never escapes from this confusion; nor do Stawski and Starosolskyj. Cf. *ibid.*, p. 18, where Ruffini takes exception to "la tendenza a confondere la maggioranza con la moltitudine, ed a colpire il principio maggioritario quando si vogliono colpire le istituzioni democratiche"!

sovereignty (*i.e.*, lodgment in the people of the power to determine the scope of its own powers) because, in the absence of such demonstration, the most he can claim for the majority is the power to have its way within the limits of the decision-making competence of the people as a whole—it being improbable that any theorist would entrust to a majority of the people a power which he would withhold from the whole. He must establish the case for popular consultation (*i.e.*, for regular expressions of the popular will) because in the absence of consultation the question whether the majority should be permitted to speak for the whole simply does not arise. And he must establish the case for *all three* because, since they constitute together the context in which he in fact proposes to apply the majority-principle, since, again, objections might well lie against majority-decisions in this context which would not lie against them in other contexts, he can enormously economize time and effort by reaching a previous understanding with his opponents on these issues. To prove the case for majority-decisions in (*e.g.*) the United States Supreme Court is not to prove the case for majority-decisions by an omnicompetent electorate which includes a large percentage of illiterates; and since it is not, he must avoid all suspicion of assimilating the two questions to one another.

These, then, are the slogans of the majority-rule democrats: formal political equality, formal popular sovereignty, techniques for discovering the (unanimous or divided) popular will, reception of majority-decisions as the equivalent of (though not necessarily equally desirable with) unanimous ones; and it is a matter of some interest that these four slogans not only *can* be separated from one another for purposes of discussion (despite the fact that all are involved in the doctrine of majority-rule), but also, because none of them by any means obviously involves any of the others, must be so separated. A man can, without inviting the charge of inconsistency, defend popular sovereignty and refuse to countenance a proposal that propertyless men and women be admitted to the suffrage. He may defend popular sovereignty and yet balk at its exercise by a mere majority of the people. He may cling to a constitution which is, in effect, a popular mandate prohibiting popular mandates, and defend it on the grounds that it *is* an exercise of popular sovereignty ("We, the people of the United States . . . . do ordain and establish,"[87] *etc.*). In the same way, a man may commit himself to formal political equality without openly abdicating his right to argue, along with Professor Friedrich, that elections are only one (and by no means necessarily the best) way of securing representative (= responsible) officials,[88] or,

[87]*Constitution of the United States*, "Preamble."
[88]Friedrich, *op. cit.*, p. 253: "It may well be that more recent experiences will lead to a reversal and a corresponding limitation of the use of electoral methods."

along with Jellinek, that "was alle beschlossen haben, kann auch nur von allen geändert werden,"[89] or, with Laski, that the time has come for us to eliminate the word "sovereignty" from our political vocabulary.[90] A man might well believe (e.g.) annual elections to be the only guarantee against tyranny, and yet insist upon (a) a majority of two-thirds of the voters as the minimum requirement for a popular mandate, (b) a "rigid" constitution limiting popular sovereignty, and (c) voting qualifications calculated to exclude much of the population from the suffrage. And, finally, a man might believe ardently in majority-decisions in plebiscites wherever plebiscites are held, and yet, with Locke, ignore the need for *machinery* for popular consultation,[91] with Pufendorf, wish to withdraw from the majority's competence (e.g.) decisions calling for expertise,[92] and, with certain California property-owners who have lately attracted the attention of the newspapers, wish to deny the vote to recipients of relief.

It would, of course, be easy to go too far in insisting upon the possibility of dealing separately with these four emphases of the majority-rule democrat's faith, precisely because they *are* emphases of a single political faith. The popular sovereignty for which the majority-rule democrat pleads is a popular sovereignty which is to be exercised by a majority of an inclusive electorate; the political equality which he demands is an equality of voting privileges in a situation where majority mandates are popular mandates and popular mandates are law; the machinery for popular consultation upon which he insists is machinery which must be judged in the light of the fact that "snap" majorities may use it to withdraw (e.g.) fundamental civil rights—or even to suppress majority-rule. In short, the case for each of the majority-rule democrat's slogans must be stated differently according as it is, or is not, stated with reference to a situation in which the others are taken for granted; and it is with reference to such a situation that the genuine majority-rule democrat will be found stating the case for these slogans.

If it were to be objected, at this point, that what the writer has done is to ascribe to the phrase "doctrine of majority-rule" an unfamiliar and quite arbitrary content, he would make his defense in the following terms:

To define the doctrine of majority-rule in this fashion (political equality plus popular sovereignty plus consultation plus majority-decisions) is, in the first place, to call out into the open, to render intelligible, and to justify an apparently illegitimate procedure of which politicists of the first rank have for a long while availed themselves. If, for example,

[89]Jellinek, *op. cit.*, p. 14.
[90]Harold J. Laski, *A Grammar of Politics* (London: George Allen and Unwin, Ltd., 1928), pp. 44-45.
[91]See below, p. 124.
[92]Samuel von Pufendorf, *De iure naturae et gentium*, vii, 2. 15: "Equidem in decidendis veritatibus theoreticis sententiae non numerantur, sed ponderantur."

the reader will turn to Jellinek's admirable *Das Recht der Minoritäten,* and examine it in the light of the foregoing discussion, he will discover that what is there put forward as an attack on the notion of decisions by majority-vote (= the majority-principle *qua* rule) is primarily, on the one hand, an attack on the notion of sovereignty (what the author calls the rights of minorities being merely *droits du citoyen* which he would like to see placed beyond all possibility of infringement by political authority of any kind), and, on the other hand, an indictment of those inclusive electorates which Jellinek, as long ago as 1896, had seen as the characteristic feature of the democracies of the future. "Die moderne Gesellschaft," he says, "befindet sich in einem immer weiter vorwärts schreitenden Process der Demokratisirung. Mag man nun diese Entwicklung mit Freude begrüssen oder fürchten, keine Macht der Welt ist imstande, diesen geschichtlichen Naturprocess dauernd zu hemmen."[93] Like Henry Adams, and, of course, many others, he regards this democratization of modern society as a "levelling" process whose end result will be the elimination not of the valleys but of the prominences in the topography of mankind[94]—as, again, a process of collectivization—in which "immer grösser wird der Antheil bemessen, den das Individuum von seiner Selbständigkeit der Gesammtheit zwangsweise zum Opfer bringen soll."[95] Both these prospects, he makes abundantly clear, are abhorrent to him in the extreme;[96] he believes that their realization, over the next one hundred years, will precipitate a major crisis in the history of civilization;[97] and he unhesitatingly identifies both tendencies with the gradual extension of the sphere of operation of the majority-principle: "Je weiter aber die Demokratisirung der Gesellschaft vorwärts schreitet, desto mehr dehnt sich auch die Herrschaft des Majoritätsprinzips aus."[98] Mankind's only hope, therefore, lies in *"Die Annerkennung von Rechten der Minoritäten."*[99]

No one, however, can read carefully these closing pages of Jellinek's famous lecture without becoming aware that his real grievance is not against the majority-principle, as he himself has defined it,[100] at all. Nothing, he insists, "kann rücksichtsloser, grausamer, den primitivaten Rechten des Individuums abholder, das Grosse und Wahre mehr hassend und verachtend sein, als eine *demokratische* Mehrheit."[101] His quarrel, therefore, lies with democratic majorities, not with majorities as such,

[93]Jellinek, *op. cit.,* p. 40.
[94]*Ibid.* The geological analogy is his. Cf. Henry Adams, *The Degradation of the Democratic Dogma* (New York: The Macmillan Company, 1919), p. 121.
[95]Jellinek, *loc. cit.*
[96]*Ibid.,* pp. 40-43.
[97]*Ibid.,* p. 43.
[98]*Ibid.,* p. 40.
[99]*Ibid.,* p. 43. Cf. Dalberg-Acton, *op. cit.,* p. 4: "The most certain test by which we judge whether a country is really free, is the amount of security enjoyed by minorities."
[100]*Ibid.,* pp. 1-2.
[101]*Ibid.,* p. 41 (italics mine).

and his reason is that he (equally, he believes, with other "realists") is disillusioned about the common man: "Nur ein der Wirklichkeit gänzlich abgewendeter Mensch kann heute noch den Traum von der Güte und Wahrheitsliebe der Massen träumen."[102] His further reason is that he believes "progress" to depend upon the recognition of a "staats- und gesellschaftsfreien Sphäre der Individuums:"[103]

Die Gefahr für die freie Entwicklung der Individualität und der Minoritäten, die ja, wie wir sahen, eng miteinander verbunden sind, ist dennoch gross genug und erscheint umso grösser, wenn man bedenkt, dass aller Fort ˙ ritt in der Geschichte seinem Ursprunge nach das Werk von Minoritäten gewesen ist.[104]

These, however, are arguments, not against decisions by majority-vote *qua* decisions by majority-vote, but against a political sovereignty which involves authority to withdraw individual rights which he regards as desirable, and against suffrage arrangements which give to the masses of men a voice in political decisions—or, what comes to the same thing, against majority-decisions where such political sovereignty and such suffrage arrangements exist and (because implemented by machinery for popular consultation) can actually affect the course of events. And this means that we must either convict Jellinek of intellectual confusion *vis-à-vis* the issue to which he was addressing himself, or plead in his defense that his confusion was merely verbal and did not lead him astray in the construction of his argument. As a matter of fact, the latter proceeds exactly as it would have done if he had defined the majority-principle as we have here defined the doctrine of majority-rule—*i.e.*, as a complete political faith capable of being broken down into several emphases, only one of which is allegiance to the notion of decisions made by majority-vote. Far from being confused intellectually, Jellinek knew perfectly well what it was that he objected to in the political tendencies of his time, and knew perfectly well what he would like to see done about it. He was, in fact, an old-fashioned philosopher of natural rights, who stood aghast at the thought that shortly individuals would have *no* rights except those vouchsafed to them by popular majorities, and felt that only in America had men learned how to guarantee those conditions in which minorities can discharge their responsibilities as the bearers of civilization. Among modern political innovations, therefore, he could bring himself to admire only the checks and balances and bills of rights and difficult processes of amendment which he found in the American constitutions—and judicial review; and he put the case for these "Minoritätenschutzen" as neatly as anyone ever has. His clear purpose, in the volume in question, is to put to rout those persons who do not recognize

---

[102]Jellinek, *op. cit.*, p. 41.
[103]*Ibid.*, p. 42.
[104]*Ibid.*

the wisdom and necessity of such restraints by attacking the whole of their political creed as he understands it; and the main points of that creed are, as may be seen from the passages we have reproduced, the slogans which we have put forward as the content of the doctrine of majority-rule. The most serious charge that will lie against him is, therefore, that he has (a) placed upon his readers the burden of formulating the creed for themselves, and (b) misled them by applying to it a term (the majority-principle) to which he has assigned a much narrower meaning.

Many writers have followed Jellinek in this respect, urging against the majority-principle objections which are in fact objections to unlimited government and political equality and the plebiscitary determination of public issues; and our point is that while this procedure appears to rest on a confusion of categories, its soundness is nevertheless guaranteed by the unity of the phenomenon (*i.e.*, majority-rule) against which (or, *mutatis mutandis*, in favor of which) they have written.

In the second place, the content here ascribed to the concept of majority-rule is neither unfamiliar nor arbitrary, since not a few reputable writers on politics can be shown to have employed the term in this sense. "We forget," wrote J. Allen Smith, "that when our government was established the principle of majority-rule was nowhere recognized—that until well along into the nineteenth century *the majority of our forefathers did not even have the right to vote*,"[105] thus reserving the term majority-rule for those situations where, as he puts it, the masses have "secured the right of suffrage,"[106] and where provision has been made for "the enforcement of public opinion in ·the management of public affairs."[107] Nor can he conceive of a majority-rule system in which the majority is hampered in its political action by constitutional limitations enforced by officials not subject to majority-control:

If the will of the majority is to prevail, the courts must be deprived of the power which they now have to declare laws null and void. Popular government can not really exist so long as judges who are politically irresponsible have power to override the will of the majority. . . . The final interpreter of the constitution must be the majority.[108]

So, too, with Edward Elliott, who, like Smith, identifies democracy with majority-rule,[109] and like Smith sought to call attention to those features of American government which are incompatible with the latter. "Bills of Rights," he says, "are sadly out of harmony with a spirit which

[105]Smith, *op. cit.*, p. 369 (italics mine).
[106]*Ibid.*
[107]*Ibid.*
[108]*Ibid.*, p. 356.
[109]Edward Elliott, *American Government and Majority Rule* (Princeton: Princeton University Press, 1916), p. 111.

demands the rule of the majority; they are a species of limitation whose *raison d'être* is gone,"[110] thus making the defenders of majority-rule accountable (as we have made them accountable) for a defense of the idea of sovereignty—a sovereignty which is, furthermore, to be exercised by an inclusive electorate[111] provided with machinery calculated "to make easy the supremacy of the will of the majority."[112] Our use of the term "majority-rule" can, therefore, be justified in terms of distinguished precedents.

[110]Elliott, *op. cit.*, p. 124.

[111]*Ibid.*, p. 60: "It was a logical result of the principle of popular rule that there should be an irresistible demand to increase the number of those who might participate in the affairs of the government."

[112]*Ibid.*, p. 132.

Chapter II

APOLOGIA FOR THE PRESENT STUDY

THE PRESENT treatise is the first of a series of monographs in which the writer proposes to trace the history of speculation about the doctrine of majority-rule, as defined in the preceding chapter, from the earliest moment at which it can be shown to have assumed the form there attributed to it, down to the present day. For reasons which are not, the writer hopes, altogether arbitrary, he has chosen the political theory of John Locke as representing that earliest moment; and the purpose of this chapter is (1) to make clear to the reader the considerations which have dictated that choice, and (2) to explain the plan upon which the study will proceed.

There is, of course, a certain artificiality involved in speaking of the "earliest moment" at which a doctrine or idea assumed a given form. As G. D. H. Cole has argued:

The form in which men cast their speculations, no less than the ways in which they behave, are the result of the habits of thought and action which they find around them. Great men make, indeed, individual contributions to the knowledge of their times; but they never transcend the age in which they live. The questions they try to answer will always be those their contemporaries are asking; their statement of fundamental problems will always be relative to the traditional statements handed down to them.[1]

Even the most startlingly original thinkers, that is to say, differ at most very little from those to whom they are indebted for the concepts they employ and the problems they seek to solve; and any talk of "earliest moments" in the history of political theory must be heard with that fact in mind. Nevertheless, it is because of these small differences between the thought of seminal thinkers and that of their contemporaries and forebears that thought has a history; and the artificiality which attaches to fixing attention upon them is an unavoidable incident of its writing. We therefore make no apology for it, but beg the reader to bear in mind the fact that what we are asserting, with respect to Locke, is simply that the writer has been able to find no earlier trace of a certain "twist" which he gave to certain traditional conceptions by combining them in a different way from his predecessors.

In other words, while the concept of equality had been present in political literature since the time of the Stoics, the concept of decisions by majority-vote since the time of Plato and Aristotle, and the concept of popular sovereignty present (in a form highly similar to that which it assumes in Locke's theory) in such a writer as Althusius, Locke (as

[1]G. D. H. Cole, "Introduction" to J. J. Rousseau, *The Social Contract and Discourses* (London: J. M. Dent & Sons, 1913), p. vii.

we seek to show in the following chapters) combines these things into a theory of political right for which the present investigator has been able to find no precedent in political literature. Whether or not that theory is sufficiently like that of the modern majority-rule democrat to justify the use here made of it is a question upon which we must entreat the reader to suspend judgment until he has read the main body of our argument; and we shall attempt nothing more, at the present juncture, than to show why no earlier writer seemed likely to serve our purpose.

The democratic idea, which alone provides a context for a theory of majority-rule (the latter being a left-wing variant of the former), had to wait upon the emergence of the idea of the modern state itself—an event which, in the history of political theory, is now associated with the name of Machiavelli.[2] It had, also, to await emancipation from the notion that questions about social and political order can be solved with quotations from the Bible, and the kindred notion (so repugnant to Rousseau) that the things of this world do not matter:

La patrie du chrétien n'est pas de ce monde. Il fait son devoir, il est vrai, mais il le fait avec une profonde indifférence sur le bon ou mauvais succès de ses soins. Pourvu qu'il n'ait rien à se reprocher, peu lui importe que tout aille bien ou mal ici-bas. Si l'État est florissant, à peine ose-t-il jouir de la félicité publique, ... Si l'État dépérit, il bénit la main de Dieu qui s'appesantit sur son peuple.[3]

Finally, democratic theory could not begin to develop until men had learned to challenge the axiom that monarchical government is the only alternative to chaos.[4]

On one or another of these grounds we may eliminate as too early for our purposes certain writers whose names suggest themselves because of distinctively "modern" elements which characterized their thought about politics. Machiavelli, though an avowed admirer of the republican institutions of Rome, reveals in the *Discourses*[5] a complete incapacity to raise seriously the question of their adaptability to the necessities of the modern state; and, though Rousseau was perspicacious enough to see in the *Prince*[6] a manual for republicans,[7] later students have failed

---

[2]Sabine, *op. cit.*, p. 351: "Machiavelli more than any other political thinker created the meaning that has been attached to the state in modern political usage. Even the word itself, as the name of a sovereign political body, appears to have been made current in the modern languages largely by his writings."

[3]Rousseau, *Contrat social*, iv. 8.

[4]Cf. C. Delisle Burns, *Political Ideals* (London: Oxford University Press, 1927), p. 143: "The Renaissance prince is not a tyrant: he is accepted by the majority as at least the less of two evils: arbitrary, non-popular, but effective government and absolute confusion." Cf. Catlin, *Story of the Political Philosophers*, p. 215: "All kings, even ungodly princes, ruled, not absolutely, but by God's will, as Paul had said, since God willed other corrupt men, in a vale of tears, to be ruled. That was a commonplace since Paul's *Epistles.*"

[5]The most convenient modern edition of the *Discorsi sopra la prima deca di Tito Livio* and of the other writings is that of G. Massoni and M. Casella, *Tutte le opere di Machiavelli* (Firenze: G. Barbèra, 1929).

[6]Even Italian writers refer to this famous work as *Il Principe*, although the correct title, which Machiavelli must have chosen to emphasize the special nature of his treatise, is *De principatibus*.

[7]Rousseau, *op. cit.*, iii. 6. In his own time Machiavelli's ambitions were doomed to disappointment because princely patrons such as the Medici could not trust a man who had not, in the *Discourses*, concealed his enthusiasm for the republican institutions of ancient Rome, but the implications which Rousseau discovered in the *Prince* seem not to have been discerned by contemporaries.

to find in it any justification for Rousseau's evident belief that its real purpose was to strengthen the hand of Demos against ambitious tyrants. The reader who approaches it without Rousseau's bias in favor of village-pump democracy will not readily attribute to its author any premise other than that peoples must choose between chaos and monarchy. Machiavelli was not only more interested in the effective exercise of sovereignty than in the concept of political right, but he clearly felt—with ample justification, no doubt—that only an authoritarian government was possible in the Italy of his day; and he was not the man to enjoy divagations in search of theoretical truths.[8]

The other great political theorist of the sixteenth century, Jean Bodin, who has been praised as the instaurator of political science because he "took the idea of sovereign power out of the limbo of theology,"[9] did indeed, in his development of that idea, in some measure approximate the conception which is involved in our doctrine of majority-rule. Sovereignty, he says, in a vocabulary to which the favorite philosopher of the French revolutionaries owes an obvious debt, is one and indivisible, unrestrained by any human power, logically incompatible with laws which cannot be set aside.[10] And, at one point in his discussion of the problems of politics, he seems willing to concede the possibility of lodging such sovereignty in a popular majority:

L'Estat populaire est la forme de Republique, où la pluspart du peuple ensemble commande en souueraineté au surplus en nom collectif, & à chacun de tout le peuple en particulier. Le principal poinct de l'estat populaire se remarque en ce que la pluspart du peuple a cõmandement, & puissance souueraine non seulement sur chacun en particulier, ains aussi sur la moindre partie de tout le peuple ensemble.[11]

But examination of Bodin's work as a whole will reveal not only that he fails to elaborate the idea and discuss it on its merits, but also that, a true son of his age, he regards it as sheer speculative fancy, sometimes on the grounds that it violates the logical requirement of an *indivisible* sovereignty:

Le principal poinct de la Republique, qui est le droit de souueraineté, ne peut estre, ny subsister, à parler propremẽt, sinõ en la Monarchie. car nul ne peut estre souuerain en vne Republique qu'vn seul: s'ils sont deux, ou trois, ou plusieurs, pas vn n'est souuerain;[12]

---

[8]Although his great contemporary, Francesco Guicciardini (*op. cit.*, 110), censures him as an impractical idealist because he hoped for political regeneration in a land so decadent as Italy.

[9]Sabine, *op. cit.*, p. 399.

[10]Jean Bodin, *Les six livres de la Republique* (Paris: Chez Jacques du Puys, 1577), i. 8. It is to be noted that in his statement of the nature of sovereignty he leaves no room for a concurrence of the subject in the will exercised by the sovereign power: "La souueraineté n'est limitee, ny en puissance, ny en charge, ny à certain temps . . . . Le poinct principal de la majesté souueraine . . . . gist principalement à donner loy aux sugets en general *sans leur consentement*" (*ibid.*, italics mine). The only limitations are the prior "lois de Dieu et de nature" (*ibid.*).

[11]*Ibid.*, ii. 7.

[12]*Ibid.*, vi. 4. He adds the practical consideration that, if sovereignty were reposed in more than one individual the inevitable consequence would be disagreement and dissension; therefore, although "les dangers de la Monarchie . . . . sont grands, ... il y a bien plus de peril en l'estat aristocratique, et plus encore en l'estat populaire" (*ibid.*). It is in the same chapter that, somewhat inconsistently, he apprehends danger from the concurrence of numbers with power in democracies: "Il n'y a point de plus dangereuse tyrannie que celle de tout vn peuple."

and sometimes on the assumption that democracy is practicable only in rude and relatively primitive societies,[13] in which the simplicity of social relationships diminishes the need for effective government. It is only to be expected, therefore, that Bodin, when he finds it necessary to advert to the majority-principle, provides no theoretical discussion of its validity in a political context, but flatly avers that it is always both noxious and unreasonable:

Les voix en toute assemblee sont comptees sans les peser; et *tousjours* le nombre des fous, des meschants et ignorants est mille fois plus grand que des gens de bien.[14]

From this he draws the conclusion that any sort of rule by the people is contrary to natural law and may therefore be disregarded in sober discussions of the government of civilized societies:

L'estat populaire est establi contre le cours, & ordre de nature, laquelle donne le commandement aux plus sages, chose incompatible au peuple.[15]

He goes so far as to deny all political competence to the majority of men:

Demander conseil au peuple, comme lon faisoit anciennement ès Republiques populaires, n'est autre chose que demander sagesse au furieux.[16]

From his summary dismissal of the whole question, it is obvious that Bodin was familiar with nothing comparable to our doctrine of majority-rule.

The Prince was written in the second decade of the sixteenth century, *The Six Books of the Republic* in the eighth. Within approximately the same period fall such influential works as Knox's *Appellation* (1558), Francis Hotman's *Franco-Gallia* (1573), Theodore Beza's *Du droit des magistrats sur les sujets* (*circa* 1574), Stephen Junius Brutus' *Vindiciae contra tyrannos* (1581), Buchanan's *De jure regni apud Scotos* (1581), Robert Bellarmine's *De potestate summi pontificis* (1610), Juan de Mariana's *De rege et regis institutione* (1599), Francisco Suárez' *Tractatus de legibus ac deo legislatore* (1612), William Barclay's *De regno et regali potestate* (1600), and James I of England's *Trew Law of Free Monarchies* (1598). The movement of ideas through the period may be described in terms of the gradual spread, from religion to politics, of the "revolutionary premise" of Martin Luther. Luther, as is well known, carefully blinded himself to the *political* implications of his revolt against ecclesiastic authority,[17] insisting always upon the Christian's duty to obey his government.[18] The first clean break with the past seems to have occurred with John Knox, who, unlike Luther, had no hope of getting the local authorities on his side in the religious controversy in which he was engaged. "It is," he wrote, "no lesse blasphemie to say, that God hath

---

[13]"Les peuples du Septentrion ou qui demeurent aux montagnes veulent les estats populaires" (*ibid.*, v. 1). In the same passage, after declaring that these peoples possess no aptitude for commerce, law, or the arts of civilization, he implies that a democracy is not a "Republique" at all.
[14]*Ibid.*, vi. 4 (italics mine).
[15]*Ibid.*
[16]*Ibid.*
[17]Sabine, *op. cit.*, p. 361.
[18]As, also, did Calvin. Cf. Catlin, *Story of the Political Philosophers*, p. 217.

commaunded Kinges to be obeyed, when they commaund impietie, than to say, that God by his precept is auctour and mentainer of all iniquitie."[19] This challenge to constituted powers is supported, however, by no reasoning that can be identified as political rather than theological, and, though Sabine finds in Knox's projected *Second Blast of the Trumpet* (1558) the elements of the doctrine that "kings owe their power to election and hence are responsible to the people for its exercise,"[20] it would be unwise to attach too much importance to a *défi* which Knox put forward on purely theocratic grounds. His fundamental postulate is the dictum that idolatry, *i.e.*, all religious forms which seem to him unauthorized by Holy Writ, must be punished by death. And since "the punishment of idolatrie doth not appertaine to kinges only, but also to the whole people," he reasons that when princes fail to discharge their obvious duty to suppress impiety, only the people remain as an instrument whereby Divinity may condignly chastise the negligent sovereign: "the People are bound . . . . to revenge to the uttermost of their power the injurie done against his [God's] Majestie."[21] It would be vain to seek in this fanaticism even the germ of a political philosophy.

Less stridently theocratic, and more reasonable in tone, are the works of Hotman, Beza, Buchanan, Junius Brutus, and Mariana, all of whom are prepared to contemplate (with, however, widely varying degrees of equanimity) the possibility of resistance to royal authority—and all of whom are interesting, for our purposes, chiefly as illustrations of how far men may go in undermining ideas upon which they have been brought up without really challenging them. Beza, for example, revives John of Salisbury's highly elusive distinction between the lawful monarch and the tyrant, and grudgingly concedes, not to people generally but to the lesser officials in any kingdom, a power to resist tyrants;[22] but for him, as for Knox, true sovereignty vests only in God, from whom kings by appointment derive eparchial authority.[23] Hotman, without for a moment raising the question whether some form of government other than monarchy (*e.g.*, a popular government) might with profit to the French people be set up in France, is concerned merely to show (by inference from an ostensibly historical account of pre-Roman and post-Roman Gaul) that the authority of the French king rests upon popular consent, as expressed through popular customs, and was never in the past regarded as absolute *vis-à-vis* those customs.[24] Despite the reputa-

[19]John Knox, *Works* (edited by David Laing, Edinburgh: For the Bannatyne Club, 6 vols., 1844-1846), IV, p. 496.
[20]Sabine, *op. cit.*, pp. 369-370.
[21]Knox, *op. cit.*, IV, pp. 504-506.
[22]Sabine, *op. cit.*, p. 377.
[23]J. W. Allen, *A History of Political Thought in the Sixteenth Century* (London: Methuen & Co., 1928), p. 315.
[24]François Hotman, *Franco-Gallia seu Tractatus isagogicus de regimine regum Galliae et de jure successionis* (Coloniae: Ex officina J. Bertulphi, 1576). Cf.: Catlin, *op. cit.*, p. 274; Sabine, *op. cit.*, p. 376; Beatrice Reynolds, *Proponents of Limited Monarchy in Sixteenth Century France* (New York: Columbia University Press, 1931).

tion of Junius Brutus as an early democrat, even the *Vindiciae* seems to contain no unambiguous statement of a truly democratic position. Any one of a half dozen meanings could with little effort be wrung from the famous declaration: "Deus reges instituit, regna regibus dat, reges eligit; populus reges constituit, regna tradit, electionem suo suffragio comprobat."[25] No greater lucidity is to be found in his famous reference to a social contract, for the equivocal statements of the author, when subjected to critical analysis, seem to lead only to the conclusion that there is no real contract at all—that "the pactum [between King and people] of the *Vindiciae* is one that cannot be cancelled even by the agreement of both parties. . . . It expresses nothing but the immutable will of God."[26]

With Mariana[27] the idea that royal authority rests upon a *contract* between king and people (present only by implication in Hotman), thus of a contractual obligation on the king's part to discharge responsibilities towards his subjects and of a contractual right on the part of the subjects to resist his authority when he fails to discharge them, takes shape as the major political innovation of the age. Mariana, with his insistence that the function of government is to minister to the needs of the governed, that the king is subject to law, and that law can be changed only by the Estates, is far more revolutionary than the author of the *Vindiciae*; and Buchanan, with his insistence that law takes its rise from the customs of the community, that royal power derives from and is limited by that law, and that the right to resist a king who exceeds his lawful authority inheres in a majority of the people,[28] is more revolutionary than either.[29] Even Buchanan, however, never emancipated himself from the notion that the problems of politics are merely the problems of monarchy. He did, indeed, develop, and to some extent expound, a concept of popular sovereignty, but he used that concept only to show that there was in the people an inalienable right to delegate governmental authority to individuals, and to recall such delegation if the monarch flagrantly violated the assumed contract:

Omnes nationes . . . . hoc communiter sentiunt, quicquid juris alicui populus dederit, idem eum justis de causis posse reposcere. Hoc civitates omnes semper jus retinuerunt.[30]

[25]In the English translation of this work (*A Defense of Liberty Against Tyrants* [with an introduction by Harold J. Laski, London: G. Bell & Sons, 1924], p. 119), this passage is rendered as follows: "It is God that does appoint kings, who chooses them, who gives the kingdom to them; now we say that the people establish kings, put the sceptre into their hands and who with their suffrages approve the election."

[26]Allen, *op. cit.*, p. 319.

[27]Juan de Mariana, *De rege et regis institutione libri tres* (Toleti: P. Rodericus, 1599). Mariana appears to have owed much to the *De principatu* of Marius Salomonius, which, according to Allen (*op. cit.*, p. 332), was published as early as 1544. The major emphasis of that work, however, seems to be legalistic, rather than political.

[28]Not, as with Junius Brutus and Mariana, in the lesser magistrates and the Estates.

[29]George Buchanan, *De jure regni apud Scotos*, the second separately-paginated part of *Opera omnia* (edidit Thomas Ruddimannus, Edinburgi: Apud Robertum Freebairn, 1715). On this interpretation of Buchanan, cf. Sabine, *op. cit.*, p. 384; Catlin, *op. cit.*, p. 272.

[30]Buchanan, *op. cit.*, p. 32.

Nor does he establish this position by arguments more solid than appeal to a consensus of opinion (*omnes sentiunt!*) which clearly did not, even at the time of writing, exist—else, surely, there had been no controversy. Buchanan equates the populus and the majority of the citizens, thus appealing to a sort of doctrine of majority-rule, but his only supporting argument for it is the tautological observation that disagreement precludes unanimity.[31] We, taught by much subsequent history, are likely to see as important in Buchanan implications which seemed negligible, or at best of purely ancillary interest, to him. Had he regarded the proposition as significant, he would have treated it more critically.

If there is so little of democratic thought in the sixteenth-century writers whom we, for one reason or another, have come to regard as the more "liberal" writers of the age, we can scarcely expect to find many considerations pertinent to our task in the works of their adversaries, whom we have come to regard as the more conservative—although, when applied to the furious polemics and daedalian logomachies of the century, these adjectives become almost as fluid and metastatic as when applied to our own times.[32] The Monarchists of the sixteenth-century had to concern themselves but little with the claims of popular government. King James neatly escapes the need for critical discussion by reckoning the logical basis of the ruler's sovereignty among the *arcana imperii,* "wherefore that which concerns the majesty of the King's power is not lawful to be disputed."[33] William Barclay insists, in his laboriously logical treatise,[34] on the indivisibility and illimitability of sovereignty, deriving all political authority from God, and flatly denying that such authority can conceivably reside even in a people which has a right to choose its ruler.

The theorists of papal supremacy offer equally little discussion of popular rights apart from religious obligations. Robert Bellarmine, concerned with establishing the supremacy of things spiritual over things temporal, recognizes the people only as an arm, as it were, of ecclesiastical authority, by which the deposition of heretic princes may be enforced.[35] And that bitter opponent of the monarchical claims to divine right, Francisco Suárez, despite his influential restatement of the political

[31]*Ibid.*, pp. 34-35. It is interesting to observe that Buchanan thought democracy appropriate to only one context, that of absolute (economic and intellectual) equality: "Natura enim justum opinior, ut, inter eos, qui caetera sunt pares, imperandi & parendi etiam vices sint pares" (*ibid.*, p. 6).
[32]We need scarcely remind the reader of the difficulty of classifying by mere dichotomy in an era in which socialism is espoused by Tories, the inalienable rights of the common man propugned by Monarchists, and the capitalist system regarded as inviolable by "Radical Socialists." On the danger of taking for granted the applicability of the concepts of one age to the historical phenomena of another, cf. Starosolskyj, *op. cit.*, p. 11.
[33]King James I, *Political Works* (edited with an introduction by Charles H. McIlwain, Cambridge: Harvard University Press, 1918), p. 169.
[34]*De regno et regali potestate* (Parisiis: Apud G. Chaudière, 1600).
[35]Allen, *op. cit.*, p. 359.

equality of men, finds in the will of God the only source of legislative authority.[36]

Despite the summary treatment made necessary by our limitations of space and purpose, we may conclude from the foregoing paragraphs that the political thought of the sixteenth century provides no *point d'appui* for a discussion of majority-rule. Although isolated gleams of "modernity" are here and there to be discerned, we may concur in Allen's conclusion that "sixteenth-century theories of sovereignty were, for the most part, fundamentally as theocratic as those of the Middle Ages."[37]

As we extend our cursory exploration into the following century, we find indeed indications that the question of popular rights obtruded itself ever more vigorously on the attention of political writers. For many decades, however, the question was neither clearly formulated nor unequivocally answered. Out of the *turba scriptorum* who, with discussions and logomachies, treatises and pamphlets, made great din in a century in which political controversy envenomed both sword and pen, there stand forth a few great writers whose works have become classics.

Before the last decade of the century, *i.e.*, before the appearance of Locke's *Two Treatises of Government*, there lived three brilliant legalistic theoreticians of whom even the most hurried survey must take notice: Johannes Althusius (*Politica methodice digesta*, 1603), Hugo Grotius (*De jure belli ac pacis*, 1625), and Samuel Pufendorf (*De jure naturae et gentium*, 1672, and *De officio hominis et civis*, 1673). To these we must add the political writings of Spinoza, and, in England, the republican theory of Harrington (*Oceana*, 1655), the radical revolutionary polemics of John Milton, and the equally radical absolutist speculation of Thomas Hobbes (*De cive*, 1642, and *Leviathan*, 1651).

The great importance of Althusius in the history of political thought has won increasing recognition in recent years, following the indagatory study by Gierke[38] and the monumental edition of the *Politica* by Friedrich,[39] although the extent of his possible influence on subsequent proponents of democracy, particularly Rousseau,[40] has not yet been fully investigated. It seems beyond question that he was employing, at a remarkably early date, some of the basic concepts of modern democratic theory, and that his discussion offers many interesting contrasts to the discussions which had taken place in the sixteenth century. Thus, in

---

[36]Suárez' book perhaps does, as Catlin observes (*op. cit.*, p. 268) make "the Jesuits the avowed nursing fathers . . . . of democracy," but the fosterling is to remain in perpetual tutelage. On the compatibility of democracy with Roman Catholicism, cf. the brilliant article by Sidney Hook, "The Integral Humanism of Jacques Maritain," *Partisan Review*, VII (1940), pp. 204-229.

[37]Allen, *op. cit.*, p. 513.

[38]Otto von Gierke, *Johannes Althusius und die Entwicklung der naturrechtlichen Staatstheorien* (Breslau: M. & H. Marcus, 1902).

[39]*Politica methodice digesta* (edited with an introduction by Carl Joachim Friedrich, Cambridge: Harvard University Press, 1932).

[40]The present writer proposes to make in the near future a study of the similarities in the doctrines maintained by Althusius and Rousseau.

Gierke's phrase, "die Politik des Althusius von der theokratischen Auffassung des Staates sich so gut wie völlig löst."[41]

, In Gierke's opinion, Althusius introduced one conception which is a *sine qua non* of all truly democratic systems of thought: "Zuerst Althusius wandte auf das dem Volke vindicirte Recht den scharfen Begriff der im Staate nur einmal vorhandenen Souveränetät."[42] In other words, here (in place of the antecedent doctrine that the people had certain rights which limited the extent of their servitude to constituted authority) we encounter a categorical affirmation that true sovereignty (*majestas*) is always resident in the *corpus symbioticum, i.e.*, in the people, and that the latter can never alienate it. They can, and in response to the dictates of human nature and social necessity do, delegate the exercise of power to administrative officers, but these officers can never be more than agents acting on the authorization of their principal. They must, therefore, enforce the will of the society. They may, on occasion, rightfully coerce its individual members, but can never coerce the society itself: "jus in singulos non in universos cives habent."[43] This, certainly, sounds very much like Rousseau; and Althusius, equally with Rousseau, is open to the charge of having elaborated a legal concept without considering the problems which its application to specific situations might present. He does not, for example, tell us whether or not a large number of individuals (*singuli*), such as a majority, can rightfully be coerced in the name of the society as a whole. But, whatever we may say of Althusius' failure to provide for a situation which may have seemed to him a remote and improbable contingency, this analysis of social obligation was a "discovery" of the first order: "Althusius als der Schöpfer einer eigentlichen theorie des contrat social betrachtet werden muss."[44]

As a matter of fact we are invited, in the course of Althusius' discussion, to contemplate a multiplicity of social contracts. By the *contractus societatis* men bind themselves together in associations, both *consociationes privatae*, such as family[45] and guild, and *consociationes publicae*, arranged in a sort of hierarchy: commune, province, and state. By their voluntary combination into the largest of these societies, the state, men delegate to that unit a power which, though revocable, is yet a power to take all necessary measures for the public good—a "potestas praeeminens et summa universalis disponendi de iis, quae universaliter ad salutem curamque animae et corporis membrorum Regni

---

[41]*Op. cit.*, p. 60.
[42]*Ibid.*, p. 144.
[43]Althusius, *op. cit.*, v. 26.
[44]Gierke, *op. cit.*, p. 99.
[45]In Althusius' valiant effort to explain the family as a legal association we may see the consequence of inordinate devotion to logical formalism, for surely the symmetry of his complex system of associations is too dearly bought when it is obtained by such distortion of one of its component parts.

seu Reipublicae pertinent."[46] This power he conceives as limited only by certain inalienable rights which natural law guarantees to the individual, and by the competence of the smaller units (from which Althusius' state is by a process of federalization constructed) to decide for themselves all matters which uniquely concern them.

The sovereign people, according to Althusius, delegates the exercise of administrative power not only to the king, or supreme magistrate, but also to the *ephors*, or lesser magistrates, each of whom has jurisdiction over a unit of the federation, and likewise acts as a member of a representative body (the council of ephors) which by majority-vote controls the supreme magistrate's administration of the federated state. Thus, although sovereignty inalienably belongs to the *corpus symbioticum*, the people appear in an active rôle only before a government is instituted and after it is dissolved. After they have (in theory) met in an assembly and formed a government, the people—without transferring their sovereignty—cease to exercise it. Their rights are subsequently protected, *vis-à-vis* the highest magistrate, by the ephors, and *vis-à-vis* the ephors, by the highest magistrate; so that a system of governmental balances is reposed on the "mutua censura et observatio inter regem et ephoros."[47] If the monarch fails to discharge his duties to his employer, the people, the *jus resistentiae et exauctorationis* is to be exercised by the ephors, who must depose him. Althusius further provides against abuse of power by the ephors by making their mandate from the people equally revocable.

This doctrine of popular sovereignty, coupled with his insistence that even the peasantry must constitute an "estate" and so exercise political power in the formation and direction of the state, lends to the *Politica methodice digesta* an appearance of great modernity, but Althusius seems never to have faced the problem of majority-rule. He is, in other words, interested in delimiting the power of officers by granting to their employers the right to dismiss them at any time, but he does not define the power of a part of the people against another part of the people. The *corpus symbioticum* is apparently an organism whose constituent parts are *ex hypothesi* substantially in harmony,[48] and a fundamental disagreement between the parts must result in fissure, *i.e.*, dissolution of the organism. But here again Althusius does not consider the possible eventualities. He does, indeed, tell us that when the chief magistrate violates the contract and is able to secure the approbation or acquiescence of a majority of the provinces (so that he cannot be deposed), the provinces unwilling to submit may, acting through their ephors, withdraw from the state and either join another federation or remain independent.[49]

---

[46] Althusius, *op. cit.*, ix. 19.
[47] *Ibid.*, xix. 109.
[48] Or, to use Althusius' terminology, every *consociatio* depends on the existence of a *communicatio concordiae*.
[49] *Ibid.*, xxxviii. 76.

This right of secession extends also to the smaller components, such as the commune. But Althusius does not answer the really interesting question, What happens when a province (or a majority of provinces) wishes to alter the terms of the contract? Does it have a right to disrupt the social aggregate by demanding to alter the terms of union? Did Althusius really contemplate a series of fissiparous and metastatic societies—one in which, for example, the "estate" of peasants might secede if its members became discontented with the conditions accorded them? And if such a right be granted to the estates, on whom falls the gravamen of the change—since a system of interpenetrating yet independent societies is scarcely conceivable? Has a *consociatio* never a right to coerce dissident members for the preservation of the whole?

That Althusius was not unaware of some of the difficulties which might flow from the right of secession is evident from the care with which he endeavors to explain[50] that the effect is merely to limit and moderate the exercise of governmental power; *i.e.*, he apparently believes that the members of a society will usually have such interests in common that they will, when faced by the prospect of a dissolution of their society, find some compromise which will enable them to avoid termination of their relationship. But he speaks of the right to secede only in connection with situations in which the social contract has been *broken*, and does not face the possibility that an equally serious situation may arise from dissatisfaction with an existing contract. Perhaps Althusius thought it improbable that such a situation would arise, for if he did debarrass himself of the mediaeval concept of the theocratic state, he had not won equal freedom from the mediaeval concept of the static state, *i.e.*, one whose structure and powers, being deduced from laws of universal validity, admit of no essential alteration. It would appear, therefore, that for all his exaltation of the sovereign people, he was thinking, in legalistic terms, of contracts which are made by the consent of *all* parties thereto,[51] and remain in force only until some one of the parties violates the covenant. In this context, the rights of individuals in a society, whether few or many (*i.e.*, a majority), may be determined by reference to the instrument of incorporation, and no *special* right is inherent in numbers. Thus the question of majority-rule cannot, and for Althusius evidently did not, arise.

The emphasis which Althusius placed on popular sovereignty has necessitated a somewhat detailed discussion of his theory, but we need devote no more than a paragraph to the better-known doctrine of Hugo Grotius; for, however interesting and suggestive its theoretical intricacies

---

[50]*Ibid.*, xxxviii. 71-75.
[51]This is the necessary consequence of Althusius' organic conception of the state. Cf. Gierke, *op. cit.*, p. 26: "Jede Verfügung über die Majestät muss daher von 'universa membra de communi consensu' getroffen werden."

may be, it clearly contains a definition of sovereignty which precludes the possibility of majority-rule. If we may appeal again to the great authority of Gierke,

Wahrend er [Grotius] die sei es reine sei es modificirte Volkssouveränetätslehre unbedingt verwart, erhob er sich, offenbar angeregt durch die gerade damals nahezu herrschende Annahme einer doppelten Majestät, zu der Ahnung des Gedankens der Staatssouveränetät.[52]

It is equally obvious that the stringent absolutism of Pufendorf[53] concedes no rights at all to a majority *qua* majority in an organized state. The very use of the term *societas inaequalis* to define a state as distinct from the *societas aequalis,* which, being a mere aggregation of persons subject to no sovereign authority other than their own will, is merely *rudimenta civitatis,* suggests the orientation of Pufendorf's thought. Although a majority of the members of a *societas aequalis* may bind all the members of that society and their posterity to a contractual submission to a supreme magistrate, not only the majority but the whole people, by becoming a *societas inaequalis,* cease both to exercise and to possess sovereignty, for by the social contract "populus ut persona moralis expiravit." From this Pufendorf, as is well known, elaborates a monarchically metaphysical state in which the will of the ruler is the general will (*voluntas civitatis*) and not even *omnes excluso Rege* can claim to represent this general will. It is not unfair to say that the only right which Pufendorf concedes to majorities is the right to abdicate.

The political philosophy of Spinoza seems at first sight more promising for our purposes. He deduces, as a consequence of the illimitability of sovereignty, the proposition that the individual, when once he has entered the state, "is no longer his own master; he is bound to obey all the commands of the sovereign authority, however unreasonable he may, in his own mind, consider them to be. . . . His individual will, in fact, is replaced by that of the community at large."[54] It is to be observed that persons are here subjected to the sovereignty of the community, *i.e.,* the people as a whole, and in this sense Gierke is justified in his statement that the theory "den allseitigen Verzicht der Einzelnen auf das Naturrecht zunächst als Unterwerfung unter die hierdurch zum einheitlichen Körper beseelte Gesammtheit auffasst und somit die übrigen Staatsformen nur als Abwandlungen der zur Normalform erhobenen Demokratie betrachtet."[55] But the concept of a communal will enables Spinoza to avoid the conclusion, which would otherwise inescapably follow from his proposition that the individual surrenders his rights to society, as, on another level, his attempt to make of politics a natural

[52]*Op. cit.,* p. 172.
[53]On Pufendorf, cf. Gierke, *op. cit.,* pp. 88-89; Catlin, *op. cit.,* pp. 430, 431.
[54]Spinoza, *ap.* C. E. Vaughan, *Studies in the History of Political Philosophy before and after Rousseau* (edited by A. G. Little, Manchester: University Press, 2 vols., 1925), I, p. 74.
[55]Gierke, *op. cit.,* p. 87.

rather than a normative science led him to place great emphasis on the *effectiveness* of a given government: "In his political theory he tried consistently to reduce rights to natural forces and to show that strong government in the long run must be good government."[56] Thus to Spinoza popular or majoritarian government must justify itself in terms of *strength* and *efficiency*, not right, and can claim only the merit that it may in certain situations exercise a greater authority and provoke less dissatisfaction (*i.e.*, maintain greater authority) than other forms of government. "The purpose of the State Spinoza . . . . finds . . . . in the maintenance of peace and security. What maintains this peace is *eo ipso* right."[57] Obviously, so pragmatic a premise cannot be reconciled with the doctrine of majority-rule as we have stated it in our first chapter.

Although the impassioned eloquence of the only Englishman who was both a great poet and a vigorous and influential politicist was displayed in defense of a republican and anti-monarchic régime, we are not astonished to find that a man of Milton's aristocratic proclivities not only formulated no doctrine of majority-rule, but, basing his thought on a system of moral absolutism, regards the approbation of majorities as essentially irrelevant. Indeed, the passion that informs the *Defensio prima* sometimes[58] leads him very close to an insistence that a majority will most probably err in its decisions. Gooch does not exaggerate when he declares that "the voice of the people was as far from sounding to Milton like the voice of God as to Metternich."[59]

One other republican of the Cromwellian era must be noticed here,[60] for, as is well known, the ostensibly Utopian *Oceana* of James Harring-

---

[56]Sabine, *op. cit.*, p. 429. The same preoccupation with forces enables Spinoza to dispense with a discussion of a community's *right* to resist oppressive legislation by the government in power. It is sufficient for him that excessive pressure on a large number of citizens *will* produce an insurrection. This consideration operates as a *practical* limitation on constituted authority. Cf. Vaughan, *op. cit.*, I, p. 77.

[57]Catlin, *op. cit.*, p. 262; cf. Vaughan, *op. cit.*, I, p. 89.

[58]See particularly the fifth chapter. This may be found in the first volume of Milton's *Prose Works* (edited by J. A. St. John, London: George Bell & Sons, 6 vols., 1904-1909). The earlier *Tenure of Kings and Magistrates*, which reveals greater sympathy for the populace, but contains no pronouncement on the rights of majorities, may be found in the second volume of this edition.

[59]G. P. Gooch, *English Democratic Ideas in the Seventeenth Century* (Cambridge: University Press, 1927), p. 206. We may, however, question the correctness of Gooch's statement (*ibid.*, p. 151) that Milton's "sacrifice of the undistinguished multitude to the natural peers of mankind" is to be attributed to his assimilation of Classical political theories. The explanation, we believe, lies deeper than that, amounting to a basic inconsistency which Sabine (*op. cit.*, pp. 511-512) has succinctly pointed out: "With a real passion for individual liberty he united contempt for the intelligence and good will of men in the mass . . . . He wholly failed to see that individual liberty is an impracticable ideal if men are unfit to be trusted with a voice in government."

[60]The writings of the political leaders and minor publicists of the Interregnum are historically interesting, and reveal tendencies of sentiment and opinion which not only illumine the conflicting demands which shaped the events of England's great revolution, but occasionally provide remarkable parallels to contemporary tendencies. But such men as Ireton, Lilburne, Hare, Hartlib, Winstanley, Vane, and Rogers, to say nothing of the horde of anonymous pamphleteers, did not elaborate political philosophies. The more religious writers sound the trump of revelation and feel no more obliged than the Hebrew prophets to base their demands on logic, while many of their more secular fellows lose themselves in invective and vituperation, substituting violence of language for divine authority. The more sober writers, even when they are not obviously producing propaganda or writing to conciliate divergent factions, concentrate their attention not on the state, but on the state of affairs in England on the particular day on which they wrote, so that their discussions are implicate with comment on the varying phases of a highly complex historical situation. The most laborious analysis could not extract from them much general theory.

ton[61] was an attempt to elaborate a complete theory of the state. The author of the "first economic interpretation of history,"[62] laying down the rule that in any stable society the allocation of political power *must* correspond to the distribution of economic resources (*i.e.*, property), and prizing stability as one of the chief excellences of a state,[63] obviously could espouse no doctrine of majority-rule without simultaneously proposing an unmitigated economic egalitarianism, if not complete communism. His estimate that a sound government in England could legitimately be based on the approbation of five thousand landowners indicates how far he was from making such a concession. In his state, in which servants and wage-earners are denied the rights of citizenship, and even the majority of citizens have only the power to veto the enactments of an aristocratic senate chosen by an elaborate system of indirect representation,[64] we may discern a desire to minimize the possibility of real majority-rule.[65]

We shall scarcely expect to find, in so staunch a proponent of the absolute, indivisible, and irrevocable sovereignty of constituted authority as Thomas Hobbes, any comfort for those who would place the direction of public affairs in the hands of a majority. He does, indeed, grant that "men who are in absolute liberty [*i.e.*, anarchy], may, if they please, give Authority to One man . . . . as well as give such Authority to any Assembly of men whatsoever."[66] But he holds that this right ceases when a government has been established:

They that have already Instituted a Common-wealth, being thereby bound by Covenant, to own the Actions and Judgements of one, cannot lawfully make a new Covenant, amongst themselves, to be obedient to any other, in any thing whatsoever, without his permission.[67]

Thus a majority (save at the moment when a society is formed) clearly has no political competence except in a state in which it is the sovereign, and hence has no right—*qua* majority—at all. In other words, as Starosolskyj has acutely observed,[68] according to Hobbes' system the majority-principle is merely an instrumentality or device, and is on an equal footing with other devices (*e.g.*, the monarchical principle) which states can adopt.

We conclude, then, that if Locke espoused the doctrine of majority-rule, he was the earliest writer to deal with it on a scale sufficiently

---

[61]Cited above, p. 20.
[62]Catlin, *op. cit.*, p. 301. Cf. Sabine, *op. cit.*, p. 501: "Harrington . . . . was not an economic materialist."
[63]Cf. Gooch, *op. cit.*, p. 248: "Harrington feels that there is no reason why a Commonwealth should not be as immortal as the stars in heaven."
[64]Briefly analyzed by Sabine (*op. cit.*, pp. 505-506), whose summary is more satisfactory than the detailed prolixity of the original. On the "librated" sovereignty of Harrington's state, see Gooch, *op. cit.*, p. 245.
[65]Cf. Sabine, *op. cit.*, p. 507: "Harrington was emphatically not a democrat either in purpose or theory."
[66]Thomas Hobbes, *Leviathan* (London: J. M. Dent & Sons, 1914), ii. 19. Cf. S. P. Lamprecht, "Hobbes and Hobbism," *American Political Science Review*, XXXIV (February, 1940), p. 49 n.: "Hobbes . . . . recognized that the sovereign may be one man, several men, or all men. What he had to say about sovereignty is quite independent of his preference for monarchy."
[67]Hobbes, *op. cit.*, ii. 18.
[68]Starosolskyj, *op. cit.*, p. 77.

ambitious to merit our attention; and we propose, in the following pages, to consult him on each of the four problems which, in our first chapter, we have shown to be involved in it. We shall devote a chapter (Chapter VI) to Locke's views on popular sovereignty, a chapter (Chapter VII) to his views on the right of the majority, a chapter (Chapter VIII) to his views on political equality, and a chapter (Chapter IX) to his treatment of the problem of popular consultation. Since, however, the conclusions at which we shall arrive in Chapters VI, VII, and VIII are sharply at variance with prevailing notions about Locke's political theory (as also with the conclusions which the writer had expected to document when he began his study of Locke), it has seemed advisable, for reasons of strategy, to raise certain questions about the validity of those notions before directing the reader's attention to the coincidence of outlook between Locke and the majority-rule democrats. For, as we point out below, current misunderstandings about the bearing of Locke's philosophy upon the debate about majority-rule must be explained less in terms of a failure to take notice of what Locke said about the problem (the relevant excerpts from his work having been frequently reproduced and commented upon in the literature of the subject) than in terms of a widely shared conviction that he simply couldn't have meant them. The persistence of this conviction is related, on the one hand, to the (partially correct) belief that the right of the majority cannot keep house, in a well-ordered mind, with individualism, natural rights, or objective moral standards, and, on the other hand, to the belief that Locke's major commitments, as a political philosopher, are to these things. We therefore attempt, in Chapters III and IV, to prepare the reader's mind for the evidence he will encounter in Chapters VI, VII, and VIII, by directing attention to the *collectivist* elements in Locke's thought, against the background of which his views on majority-rule appear less flagrantly incomprehensible than they have always seemed to those who have taken account only of its individualist emphases. In Chapter V we lay bare the source of Locke's indecision (as between the collectivist and the individualist views of society) by examining in detail his treatment of the law of nature, and by calling attention to certain inconsistencies in his account of it. In Chapter IX we discuss the major divergence between Locke's political philosophy and that of more recent majoritarians, namely, his cavalier disregard for the problem of providing institutional implementation for that right of the majority which (as we believe) takes, as our study proceeds, increasingly distinct shape as Locke's *real* answer to the problem he sets himself at the beginning of his major work on government. The argument of these nine chapters involves, to be sure, a certain vindication of the current view that, on his own principles, Locke could not have supported majority-rule. One of the central difficulties of his position (as we present it) will be shown to lie in the fact that, having asserted that subjection to personal authority is illegitimate, he subsequently ignores the truth that majorities, no less than minorities and dynasties, are made up of *persons,* who do not, *ceteris paribus,* by becoming members of a majority divest themselves of the (all too human) tendency to use their power (over individuals and minorities) selfishly. In this sense, at least, we shall concede that Locke's enunciation of the doctrine of majority-rule is a violation of his own principles. But we shall not attempt, on these grounds, to explain it away.

If our study ended with Chapter IX it would leave Locke's theory, so to speak, "up in the air"—*i.e.,* precisely where (in the opinion of the present writer) Locke's critics have hitherto been content to leave it. Previous accounts of Locke's theory have, that is to say, been indefinite with respect to the most interesting question which we can raise about any political theory, namely: What is its practical bearing? Like many current definitions of democracy, these accounts speak both of individual rights and of decision-making power in the hands of the majority, without giving any indication as to which is to take precedence over the other in case of a conflict between them. Assuming that (in a democracy, or in Locke's system) *some* rights inhere in individuals as a matter of course, who is to say what those rights are? Assuming that (in a democracy, or in Locke's system) there are certain rights which the majority cannot rightly withdraw from their individual subjects, does the democratic, or the Lockean, solution forbid exercise by the numerical majority of the power to define those rights[69]—or does it not? And if it does, where does that power rightly reside? Those who, in defining democracy, refuse to identify it with unlimited majority-rule, are, we submit, left with no unequivocal answer that they can give to the last of these questions; and so, too, are those who refuse, in describing Locke's political system, to equate it with unlimited majority-rule. They leave it, as we have already suggested, "up in the air."

We are not, be it noted, denying that both elements, indefeasible individual rights (which are, of course, only a shorthand expression for objective moral standards) and decision-making power in the majority, are present in Locke's system. Our point is that Locke would entrust to the majority the power of defining individual rights, and that the question of how a man who insists upon objective moral standards can

---

[69]We assume here—what is apparently more obvious to the writer than to the friends with whom he has discussed the problem—that the notion of rights which the majority has no right to withdraw, and the notion of lodging power in the hands of the majority to say what rights are of that nature, are not obviously incompatible. *I.e.,* it is true of governing majorities as of governing minorities and governing monarchs, that their conduct is limited *on one side* by their own standards of right and wrong, true, too, that these standards provide guarantees (of a kind) for the governed. The question whether the standards of popular majorities provide *adequate* guarantees for individuals and minorities is one that the writer would not lightly answer in the affirmative, but it is not a *question mal posée.*

have brought himself to adopt a frankly majoritarian position is itself one which demands attention. In Chapter X, which we entitle "The Latent Premise," we address ourselves to this question, and put forward (with, as we hope, all necessary caution) an hypothesis regarding the inarticulate premise which enabled Locke (in common with many another majority-rule democrat) to attempt—with an apparently clear conscience —to have it both ways with rights and majorities.

It would, in the light of this account of the direction in which the present study will move, be less than candid to describe it as *merely* a report of what Locke had to say about our doctrine of majority-rule. With a reluctance which is amply guaranteed by the prestige and authority of the critics with whom he has been obliged to take issue, the writer here puts forward what (as he is well aware) *malgré lui* has become a *reassessment* of Locke's position in the history of political philosophy. If it were to be objected that no such reassessment was needed, that there is a strong presumption against anyone's having found, at this late date, anything new in an author whose political writings have been available to students for many generations, and that, in any case, the verdict of the many patient studies which have been devoted to Locke's political theory in the past is not lightly to be set aside, he would make the following answers:

(a) The reassessment here put forward is one to which the writer has been driven by careful examination of Locke's own language, and, though possibly incorrect, it has *not* been lightly made. For the rest, the question as to whether or not it is possible to turn up something new in a "classic" which students of politics have been reading for a couple of centuries is one which must be decided on the evidence rather than on the basis of *a priori* calculation of probabilities.

(b) Although Locke's political writings have indeed been readily accessible through many generations, it would be easy (if we may judge from the bibliographies) to exaggerate the amount of intensive analysis they have received at the hands of professional students of law and politics. "Locke's *Essay on Civil Government*," wrote Sir Frederick Pollock more than two hundred years after its publication,

is well-known, and is probably the most important contribution ever made to English constitutional law by an author who was not a lawyer by profession; certainly there is nothing to be compared to it until we come to Bagehot in our own time. Still I do not know that it has ever been analysed by an English lawyer with reference to its immediate purpose and circumstances. *In fact Locke's political doctrine holds quite a secondary place in such accounts of Locke as are generally current in the hands of the educated public.*[70]

As recently as 1918 Professor Lamprecht wrote that it was the purpose of his book on Locke's moral and political philosophy "to supply a lack

---

[70]Sir Frederick Pollock, "Locke's Theory of the State," *Proceedings of the British Academy*, 1903-1904, p. 237 (italics mine).

in the existing discussions,"[71] and, though he could point to one previous monograph on Locke's ethics—M. M. Curtis' *Outline of Locke's Ethical Philosophy*—he had found none on Locke's politics.[72] "Locke," he observes, "has always held an important place in all histories of modern philosophy. . . . [Nevertheless] his moral theories, and to some extent his political theories, have been . . . . neglected."[73]

Paradoxically, it is Locke's very importance in the history of modern philosophy which seems to provide the readiest explanation for this phenomenon. "*The Essay on Civil Government*," Pollock explains, "has been overshadowed by the *Essay on Human Understanding* and the *Letters on Toleration*";[74] and Lamprecht, who accepts this conclusion, continues:

It has been his epistemology to which attention has been chiefly directed. . . . Such disproportionate emphasis upon one phase of his contribution to philosophy is not altogether surprising. Epistemological problems have been the storm center of controversy both in England and Germany ever since the *Essay concerning Human Understanding* precipitated them in so striking a form.[75]

For a long while, that is to say, students of Locke's philosophy were so busy digesting the problems which he posed regarding "the inevitable limits of human knowledge, and its validity and value within those limits,"[76] that they had little time left for study and analysis of his political writings; and, while such an explanation of the relative neglect of the latter might easily be pressed too far, and by no means accounts for the failure of critics more interested in politics than in epistemology to turn their attention to Locke's *Two Treatises*, it throws some welcome light on the fact that the latter have been—as compared with, *e.g.*, Rousseau's *Contrat social*—little written about.

Whatever the explanation of the phenomenon we have just mentioned may be, the present writer can only corroborate Sir Frederick Pollock's and Professor Lamprecht's report on the condition of the literature on Locke's politics, with the additional observation that neither of them may properly be said to have filled the bibliographical lacuna in question. Lamprecht's study is invaluable as an account of Locke's ethics; but his Book III, entitled "The Social and Political Philosophy of John Locke," by no means measures up, either as exposition or criticism, to the sustained excellence of the earlier parts of his study. Pollock can, at most, be said to have exploited to the fullest extent the possibilities of a brief

---

[71]S. P. Lamprecht, *The Moral and Political Philosophy of John Locke* (New York: Columbia University Press, 1918), p. iii.

[72]*Ibid.*

[73]*Ibid.*, p. 1.

[74]Pollock, *loc. cit.*

[75]Lamprecht, *loc. cit.* It is interesting to notice, in connection with what we have said in the preceding section (a), that not a little of the controversy precipitated by the *Essay* has turned upon the question of what Locke meant to say in it. Cf. A. Campbell-Fraser, "John Locke as a Factor in Modern Thought," *Proceedings of the British Academy*, 1903-1904, p. 225: "Opposite interpretations were put upon its central thesis, by Stillingfleet and Leibniz, in Locke's lifetime; afterwards by Voltaire and Condillac in France, by Reid and Stewart in Scotland; more recently by Coleridge, Cousin, and Green among the many who read the *Essay* as an expression of incoherent sensuous empiricism, and by Webb and Tagart, as well as recent foreign critics, who lay stress on its implied recognition of intuitive reason."

[76]Lamprecht, *loc. cit.*

lecture before a learned society; and while here, as always, he brings to bear upon his problem a store of learning and wisdom which the subsequent investigator must envy and admire, he would have been the first to agree that his treatment of it was less than exhaustive. During the years that have elapsed since Pollock's lecture, innumerable brief discussions of Locke's political theory have found their way into books on other subjects, and, of course, into such new histories of political philosophy as have seen the light of day. Of these, the most ambitious is the chapter on Locke in Vaughan's posthumous *Studies in the History of Political Philosophy,* to which (as, also, to Lamprecht's study) we shall refer frequently below. But the authors of these discussions have followed unquestioningly in the beaten path of Locke interpretation; and we may say of the *Essay Concerning the True Original, Extent and End of Civil Government* (with which we are to deal in the following chapters) what Campbell-Fraser has said of the *Essay Concerning Human Understanding*:

For a long time [it] . . . . has been spoken about more than studied; and some, even historians of [political] philosophy, have dealt with it largely at second hand, or at least *without that candid comparison of the parts with the spirit and design of the whole which is needed in the case of a book that approaches high questions in the inexact language of common life.*[77]

And, that being the case, there is, properly speaking, *no* presumption against a tardy investigator's turning up something new in it.

(c) Our reassessment of Locke's theory—if valid—has implications which are not without practical importance. The name of Locke, associated as it is in men's minds with such values as tolerance, freedom of inquiry, love of truth, *etc.,* has become a *symbol* in the continuing struggle for power under the American constitution; and, as such, has been extremely useful to those who prefer government by judiciary to majority-rule.[78] We are not suggesting, we hasten to add, that the tide of battle would long ago have turned against judicial review but for the prestige of Locke's name, or even that the course of the struggle would have been perceptibly different had Locke's name not been used as a weapon in it. But no one who is aware of the amount of energy which has been devoted to the task of "proving" that the framers of the constitution of the United States intended that document to provide for judicial review[79] will question the fact that men of an extremely practical turn of

---

[77]*Ibid.* (italics mine).

[78]Just as the name of Rousseau, associated as it is in men's minds with sentimentality, state-worship, and the complete subjection of the individual to his society, has been hurtful to the cause of those who prefer majority-rule to government by judiciary. While in the text of the following chapters we avoid the problem as much as possible, we shall devote occasional footnotes to the purpose of establishing a *prima facie* case in favor of a parallel reassessment of Rousseau's position. His language, like Locke's, offers little justification for the use to which his name has been put in this connection. For a typical instance of that use, cf. C. J. Friedrich, *op. cit.,* p. 481.

[79]Another interesting example is what Sidney Hook calls the "Kampf um Marx"—the dispute, among the different branches of the socialist movement, as to which has the clearest title to the adjective "Marxist," thus the clearest title to exploit the symbolic value of Marx's name.

mind *do* attach importance to such considerations—and our point is that
those who have sought to associate the framers of the constitution with
judicial review have had a comparable interest in establishing the association of ideas (on which we have all been brought up) between the
framers and John Locke, thus, ultimately, between judicial review and
Locke's theory of natural rights. If, as we argue below, Locke's natural
rights are merely the rights vouchsafed by a legislature responsible to
the majority, the opponents of judicial review can easily capture for
themselves a symbol which might prove extremely useful.

Less important from a practical point of view, but equally interesting,
are the implications of our interpretation of Locke with respect to the
official account of his "influence"—not only upon the authors of the
Declaration of Independence and the framers of the constitution, but
also upon the broad sweep of American political theory. It would be
easy to document the statement that the *Second Treatise* has, beyond any
other European work on politics, affected the character and tendency of
this phase of American thought; and, if the present writer had found in
Locke the (ultimately) anti-majoritarian emphasis which he had been
led to expect, this Introduction would, no doubt (in view of the dearth of
majoritarian theory in the United States), have exploited this possibility
to the fullest extent. Since, however, the proposition that such-and-such
a writer was profoundly influenced by Locke almost always turns out
to mean that the writer in question said things which bear a greater or
lesser resemblance to what Locke is supposed to have said,[80] and since
the thesis of the present study is precisely that Locke did not *say* the
things he is supposed to have said, we are obviously in no position to
insist upon the importance of Locke's influence upon American ideas.
That this is not unfair to the available documentation on Locke's influence
in this country, that, too, the thesis of the present study raises interesting
questions regarding the accuracy of the things we are accustomed to read
about Locke's influence in America, may be seen from the following
excerpt from so careful a writer as Vernon Parrington:

James Kent, whose long life and ripe legal learning were devoted to upholding
what he conceived to be the ultimate principles of law and politics, was the chief
thinker of the transition days of New York. A disciple of Locke and Blackstone,
remodeling seventeenth-century liberalism into eighteenth-century conservatism,
he was concerned to erect the barriers of the Common Law about the unsurveyed
frontiers of the American experiment, *assigning exact metes and bounds beyond*

---

[80]Our point is that it would be desirable to speak of "influence" only where (as, *e.g.*, in
the relation between Rousseau and Kant) there is evidence not only that the later writer thought
what the earlier writer thought, but also that he came to think as he did as a result of the
earlier writer's persuasiveness—or, at least, that the later writer had actually read the earlier.
Cf. Francis G. Wilson, *The Elements of Modern Politics* (New York: McGraw-Hill Book Co.,
1936), p. 120: "When we recall the fact that the Supreme Court of the United States still
refers occasionally to the 'social compact' and that it still thinks of 'fundamental rights,' it is
not difficult to grasp the tremendous historical significance of the political ideas of Locke."
But cf. *ibid.*: "The theory of Locke had a profound influence on American political thought.
While Jefferson read the works of the great Cardinal Belarmine, *he read more intensely the
English thinkers, notably Locke*" (italics mine).

which it should not go. Like John Marshall and Joseph Story *he was expert in devising legal springes to catch unwary democrats,* and while the Jeffersonians were shouting over their victories at the polls, he was engaged *in the strategic work* of placing the Constitution under the narrow custodianship of the English law.[81]

For (as we show below) Blackstone, whose name Parrington links with Locke's, objected to Locke's theory on precisely the grounds that it did *not* assign metes and bounds to popular government (or set springes for unwary democrats)—and it is to Story that we shall have to turn, at the end of our study, for the most extreme enunciation of the doctrine of majority-rule that is to be found in the (post-Lockean) literature of the subject!

It remains to add that the writer's chief purpose, in the following chapters, is neither to reassess Locke's position in the history of political theory nor to discover what he had to say about the four problems involved in the doctrine of majority-rule—the two purposes which he has, thus far, avowed—but to throw what light he can upon the much wider, much more important question of whether or not that doctrine can be defended upon rational grounds. The reader will, he hopes, bear this in mind as he finds his way through several lengthy critical discussions which would be quite out of place in a study of primarily historical orientation.

---

[81]Vernon Louis Parrington, *Main Currents in American Thought* (New York: Harcourt, Brace and Company, 3 vols., 1927), II, pp. 197-198 (italics mine). If Parrington had read Locke as closely as he read other writers, he would have known that Locke carefully defined "property" to include life and liberty as well as estate, and would not have helped to give currency to the following misapprehension about Locke's "influence": "[Kent] accepted the dictum of Locke that 'the great and chief end . . . . of men's uniting into commonwealths, and putting themselves under government, is the preservation of their property'; and believing that the English Common Law was the securest of all agencies devised to safeguard the subject in the enjoyment of his property rights, he made no difficulty in imposing that law upon the Constitution" (*ibid.*). Cf. *ibid.*, I, p. 189, where Parrington sets down what he takes to be the gist of Locke's theory.

PART TWO

LOCKE'S DOCTRINE
OF MAJORITY-RULE

CHAPTER III

THE PRINCE OF INDIVIDUALISTS

IF A PLEBISCITE were to be conducted among contemporary students of political theory in order to discover—*via* majority-rule procedures—their collective opinion as to whether or not John Locke was an extreme majority-rule democrat, it seems highly probable that the vote would be in the negative. Locke is one of those political philosophers whom the enterprising scholar may safely expound without becoming personally acquainted with his writings. His thought has long since been summarized by critics and historians who can hardly be supposed to have misrepresented it; and those summaries clearly show him to have been a theorist who *on his own principles* could not have advocated unrestricted majority-rule. Rousseau is another such philosopher; of his thought also we possess summaries, and since these reveal him as a man who *on his own principles* could not have advocated anything except unrestricted majority-rule, a vote about his claim to the title of extreme majority-rule democrat would almost certainly produce the opposite result.[1] They are both accounted writers upon whom we could depend—if ever (in the phrase which Morris Cohen[2] applies to Rousseau alone) we were to "take the unusual course of actually reading [them]"—not to say anything surprising on the subject of majority-rule.

According to the current summaries,[3] Locke is, above all, the "prince of individualists,"[4] the philosopher of those individual rights of which no man can (even if he chooses to) divest himself, the exponent of that ultimate "right of revolution" to which minorities may—with the approval

[1]Cf. Friedrich, *Constitutional Government*, pp. 340-341: "One hundred and fifty years ago, the theory of abstract democracy reached its abstract perfection in the glittering generalizations of Jean-Jacques Rousseau. The great French Revolution, as well as the dictatorship of the First Napoleon, is anticipated in its brilliant passages about the unlimited power of the sovereign majority . . . . No wonder that Communism, Fascism, as well as Bonapartism, should have felt satisfied when assured approximate majority support." In fairness to Professor Friedrich, it should be noticed that he has subsequently reinterpreted Rousseau, and found him to be an exponent of rule by qualified majorities. He writes now ("One Majority Against Another," *Southern Review*, V [1939], p. 45): "Does Rousseau mean by a majority a majority of one [an 'approximate' majority]? Far from it." Cf. Saripolos, *op. cit.*, p. 213: "Rousseau se rendait parfaitement compte de l'inadmissibilité *théorique* et des dangers pratiques de la loi de majorité quant à la liberté et la souveraineté des citoyens. Voilà pourquoi il voulait . . . . restreindre, autant que possible, les applications de cet expédient injustifiable en droit." We shall attempt, in occasional footnotes through the following pages, to throw some light upon Rousseau's position with regard to majority-rule.

The view now current in academic circles regarding the respective positions of Locke and Rousseau on the question of majority-rule emerges very clearly in the following passage from Eduard Heimann, *Communism, Fascism, or Democracy?* (New York: W. W. Norton & Co., 1938), pp. 54-55: "Since the minority is a part of the people, the merger of . . . . two principles is logically necessary and has always suggested itself much more readily in history than the reconciliation of *the two underlying philosophies developed by Rousseau on the one hand and by Locke and Montesquieu on the other*. Both ways must be combined in any modern image of democracy; we have come to regard majority governments working under elaborate constitutional limitations as the only adequate form of political democracy" (italics mine).

[2]Cohen, *op. cit.*, p. 402.

[3]Cf., for a typical example, Vaughan, *op. cit.*, I, pp. 130-203. Summaries of the kind the writer has in mind are to be found in all the standard works on the history of political theory.

[4]*Ibid.*, I, p. 156.

of all reasonable men—make their appeal when majorities grow tyrannical. Locke "begins" by positing the existence of a state of nature, the
distinguishing feature of which is the complete absence of organized
government. Hobbes, before Locke, had held that in their natural state
men were engaged in a war of all against all; and Locke, against Hobbes,
held that—save for an occasional supervention of a "state of war"—
their natural condition was one of peace and goodwill. Hobbes, before
Locke, had held that such things as "rights" and "property" are incon-
ceivable in the state of nature, and can arise only after man's entrance
into civil society; Locke, against Hobbes, held that men in the state of
nature are the subjects of certain *natural* rights, *e.g.*, "to order their
actions, and dispose of their possessions and persons as they think fit
. . . . without asking leave or depending upon the will of any other
man."[5] Respect for these rights Locke conceived to be enjoined by a law
of nature, "as intelligible and plain to a rational creature and a studier
of that law as the positive laws of commonwealths, nay, possibly plainer.
. . . ."[6] And, but for the inconvenience of having no common judge or
superior to whom disputes arising under the law of nature might be
referred, Locke thought men might well have chosen to remain in the
state of nature indefinitely:

If man in the state of Nature be so free as has been said, if he be absolute lord
of his own person and possessions, equal to the greatest and subject to nobody,
why will he part with his freedom, this empire, and subject himself to the dominion
and control of any other power?[7]

There being no common judge, however, their rights were not in fact
secure, and in the fullness of time men did become willing to emerge
from the state of nature into the civil state. Since, however, one of the
rights which each possessed in the state of nature was that of being
bound only by his own consent, the transfer could be accomplished only
by means of a compact. They therefore agreed together to establish a
common superior to decide disputes between them, and the state of
nature (as between the parties to the compact) ceased. Locke is, as the
summaries present him, very clear as to the purposes of the compact:
"The great end of men's entering into society [is] . . . . the enjoyment
of their properties [= their rights] in peace and safety."[8] They entered
"*only* with an intention in every one the better to preserve himself, his
liberty and property (for no rational creature can be supposed to change
his condition with an intention to be worse)."[9] Furthermore, the form
of the compact must not violate that further provision of the law of

---

[5]John Locke, *Essay Concerning the True Original, Extent and End of Civil Government*
(reprinted in *Of Civil Government* [edited by William S. Carpenter, London: J. M. Dent &
Sons, 1936], pp. 117 ff.), ii. 4. In subsequent citations of this work, we shall give only the
chapter and section numbers (according to this edition).
[6]ii. 12.
[7]ix. 123. Why indeed?
[8]xi. 134.
[9]ix. 131 (italics mine).

nature according to which "a man, not having the power of his own life, cannot by compact or his own consent enslave himself to any one, nor put himself under the absolute, arbitrary power of another."[10] The "common superior" which resulted from the compact accordingly possesses powers of a highly limited character. It has only the power which the parties to the compact assigned to it—*i.e.*, a power which was defined beforehand in the light of that *sole* intention of the parties to preserve themselves and the liberties which they enjoy under the law of nature:

It is a power that hath *no other end* but preservation, and therefore can never have a right to destroy, enslave, or designedly to impoverish the subjects; the obligations [thus also the "rights"?] of the law of Nature cease not in society, but only in many cases are drawn closer, and have, by human laws, known penalties annexed to them to enforce their observation. Thus the law of Nature [thus also natural rights?] stands as an eternal rule to all men, legislators as well as others. The rules that they make . . . . must . . . . be conformable to the law of Nature—*i.e.*, to the will of God.[11]

The common superior created by the compact is not, therefore, "sovereign" in any intelligible sense of that word; sovereignty, as in *Lochner* vs. *New York*,[12] belongs to individual rights and to that law of nature (or constitution) which defines them. The summarizers can (and do), therefore, take cognizance of Locke's assignment of *some* decision-making power to the majority without giving rise to any confusions between Locke's position and the position of that absolutist of majority-rule, Jean-Jacques Rousseau. The majority is to make decisions, but its competence is bounded on all sides by the "inalienable" rights of individuals and minorities. The majority cannot withdraw these rights, since if it were to withdraw them it would be exercising over the minority a power which the latter, under the law of nature, could not rightfully have given up.

Such is, we suggest, the theory attributed to Locke by most recent writers on political philosophy. It is, admittedly, a theory which leaves no room for the doctrine of majority-rule as defined in our Introduction; it is, again, one which contains no surprises for the American student who knows that Locke was the favorite philosopher of the authors of the American Revolution,[13] who expects as a matter of course to find in Locke the basic principles of the form of government which has obtained in the United States since that revolution, who knows, finally, that Locke's real purpose in inventing his theory was to "justify" the Revolution of 1688—a revolution which, on anybody's showing, postponed until the nineteenth century, or until the twentieth, or until the Greek kalends, the erection in England of a system of genuine majority-rule. It is a theory which coincides nicely with the doctrines emphasized by the same writer

[10]iv. 22.
[11]xi. 135 (italics mine).
[12]198 U. S. 45 (1905), where it was held that a maximum-hour law for bakers was an "unreasonable, unnecessary and arbitrary interference with the right and liberty of the individual baker to contract in relation to labor." Cf. *Coppage* vs. *Kansas*, 236 U. S. 1 (1915).
[13]Parrington, *op. cit.*, I, p. 189.

in the *Letters on Toleration*. It is a theory which, by regarding society as a collection of "atomistic," *i.e.*, discrete individuals, does precisely what we should expect from the gifted author of the *Essay Concerning Human Understanding*. It is a theory which lends itself to ready documentation with apparently unambiguous passages from *An Essay Concerning the True Original, Extent and End of Civil Government*.[14] It can, nevertheless, be shown to bear no relation whatever to the central argument of that essay; and it must be dissociated from Locke's name if we are ever to understand the *real* significance of the *Second Treatise* in the modern debate about majority-rule.

The truth of the matter is that Locke did *not* "begin" with individuals in a state of nature, but with a definition of political power so authoritarian and collectivist in its bearing that no genuine individualist (*e.g.*, Rousseau) could conceivably accept it:

Political power, then, I take to be a *right* of making laws, with *penalties of death*, and consequently all less penalties for the regulating and preserving of property, and of employing the force of the community in the execution of such laws, and in the defence of the commonwealth from foreign injury, *and all this only for the public good*.[15]

He *puts* men into the state of nature (in Chapter II) in order to provide himself with a *locus standi* from which to survey societies in which such power exists (Locke having been aware that he who would understand such a society must first "think" himself outside it).[16] He speaks, sometimes, *as if* men in the state of nature were discrete individuals—partly, perhaps, to make his theory more intelligible to readers of Hobbes[17] (who *had* thought in terms of discrete individuals), partly, perhaps, as a concession to the uncompromising nominalism of his epistemology.[18] But, as will be shown below, his discrete individuals always prove, upon examination, to be the highly socialized individuals whom he had in mind when he wrote (*e.g.*) his parting words about the commonwealth,[19] and the rights he claims for them, even in the state of nature, are rights which have their origin in social needs. And as for his having set out merely to "justify" the Revolution of 1688, here it is Locke's word against that of the historians:[20]

---

[14]To which we shall subsequently refer as the *Second Treatise*.
[15]i. 3 (italics mine). Cf. iv. 22: "Nobody can give more power than he has himself, and he that cannot take away his own life cannot give another power over it." Cf. vii. 86, where he concludes that the family is *not* a commonwealth because it involves no "legislative power of life and death."
[16]See below, p. 75.
[17]See below, p. 77.
[18]Cf. Lamprecht, *op. cit.*, p. 53.
[19]xix. 243.
[20]And, unless we read more carefully than most of Locke's critics, against his own. The exact language of the relevant passage of the Preface to the *Two Treatises* (which Professor Carpenter has unaccountably omitted from his otherwise eminently satisfactory edition) is as follows: "to establish the Throne of our great Restorer, Our present King WILLIAM; to make good his *Title in the Consent of the People*" (*Two Treatises of Government* [London: For Awnsham Churchill, 1690], f. A3ʳ, italics mine). An age which has become accustomed, as ours has, to consensual explanations of political authority, too easily overlooks the significance which the last ten words must have possessed for Locke's early readers—and for Locke himself. Cf. Lamprecht, *op. cit.*, p. 141: "He was primarily concerned with writing an apologetic for the

He that will not give just occasion to think that all government in the world is the product only of force and violence, and that men live together by no other rules but that of beasts, where the strongest carries it, ... must of necessity find out another rise of government, another original of political power, and *another way of designing and knowing the persons that have it* than what Sir Robert Filmer hath taught us.[21]

This is only another way of stating the problem which Rousseau set for himself;[22] and it removes Locke's *Second Treatise* from the category of *livres de circonstance* (where the historians have sought to place it) into that of books which set out to solve the basic questions of political theory. However unsatisfactorily, Locke did solve them, and *his solution is, at every point except one, that of the majority-rule democrats.* So long as he continues to be regarded as the philosopher of individual rights *against* the majority, much remains to be done to put straight the record regarding the modern debate about majority-rule. For he is captain of one of the two opposing teams.

---

form of government which came into being under William III." Cf. R. I. Aaron, *John Locke* (London: Oxford University Press, 1937), p. 272: "The immediate aim [of the *Second Treatise*] is apparent: to justify the Revolution of 1688 . . . . But this aim is achieved by securing in turn *a great and fundamental political principle,* true for the English nation in 1688 and true, in Locke's opinion, for all well-regulated communities everywhere and at all times" (italics mine).

[21]i. 1 (italics mine).

[22]Cf. Rousseau, *Contrat social,* I *prae* 1: "Je veux chercher si, dans l'ordre civil, il peut y avoir quelque règle d'administration légitime et sûre." Note, however, that Locke does and Rousseau does not beg the question whether a right to political power *can* inhere in specific persons. Cf. R. M. MacIver, *Community* (London: Macmillan and Co., 1920), p. 423: "The whole attempt to identify the principle of democracy—as any other political principle—with that of morality is fore-doomed to failure."

CHAPTER IV

THE DOCTRINE OF INALIENABLE RIGHTS

ALTHOUGH the passages reproduced in the preceding chapter are indeed from the *Second Treatise,* no close reader of that book will find it easy to understand how Locke ever got his reputation as a defender of the notion of "inalienable" individual rights. The word "inalienable," for example, does not appear to be his; and while he speaks often enough of rights (as also of freedom, liberty, liberties), we are certain to miss Locke's meaning altogether unless we understand that the "law of Nature" which confers them[1] is a law which imposes duties as well—an imposition regarding which theories of inalienable rights are notoriously silent. While, for example, a man in Locke's state of nature may indeed do what he will with himself and his own (*i.e.,* he has a "right" to do what he will with himself and his own), the exercise of that right must not involve a violation of that law of nature which he is "under," which confers the right, and which alone obligates others to respect it.[2] The law of nature enjoins, among other things, "equality" (= absence of sub-ordination), thus, constructively, a "right" not to be subordinated; but the paragraph in which the injunction is discussed makes this right merely the correlate of a duty not to subordinate others;[3] and we are told in the following lines that the natural law of equality is the "foundation of that obligation to mutual love amongst men on which [are built] . . . . *the duties they owe one another.*"[4] Furthermore, Locke's treatment of these duties shows that he regards their performance as the source of the individual's right to order his actions and dispose of his possessions and person as he thinks fit, their non-performance as adequate reason for withdrawal of that right. Anticipating the objection that his state of nature is one in which men are conceived as enjoying rights without performing the corresponding duties, Locke writes:

That all men may be restrained from invading others' rights, and from doing hurt to one another, and the law of Nature be observed, ... the execution of the law of Nature is in that state put into every man's hands, whereby every one has a right to punish the transgressors of that law to such a degree as may hinder its violation. For the law of Nature would, as all other laws that concern men in this

---

[1] ii. 4.
[2] *Ibid.*
[3] *Ibid.* Cf. vi. 56-74, where he makes the right of parents over children a function of their duties to them, and views it as the obverse of a duty on the part of the children to obey.
[4] ii. 5 (italics mine). Locke professes to be indebted for this notion to Hooker, who, however, in the passage cited, proceeds unashamedly to make of the obligation to perform the duties in question merely a good bargain: "If I cannot but wish to receive good, even as much at every man's hands, as any man can wish unto his own soul, how should I look to have any part of my desire herein satisfied, unless myself be careful to satisfy the like desire? . . . . If I do harm, I must look to suffer, there being no reason that others should show greater measure of love to me than they have by me showed unto them." Locke nowhere actually commits *himself* to this explanation.

world, be in vain if there were nobody that in the state of Nature had a power to execute that law, and thereby preserve the innocent and restrain offenders.[5]

The individual's rights cannot, therefore, be made an excuse for violating the body of law which defines them, or for shirking the *social duties* which it imposes. (Even the right to reparation for damages—so fundamental with Locke that he almost permits himself to say that it *cannot* be withdrawn in civil society[6]—appears in this context as the correlate of a duty to make reparation for damages which one has inflicted.) They cannot be because Locke is thinking in terms of an inherent right in the community to withdraw rights from individuals who do not perform the duties which attach to them. Such a view of rights and duties can, however, be pressed—and Locke certainly presses it—only at the cost of conceding that rights do not inhere in the individual *qua* individual at all, but rather in the individual as related to other individuals in a community whose *characteristicum* is a complex of reciprocal rights and duties; at the cost, again, of conceding that rights are inalienable only in the sense that duties are inalienable—thus, as any man knows who has failed at some time to perform a duty, not inalienable at all.

How far Locke actually was from entertaining the individualistic views often attributed to him in this connection may readily be gathered from his ideas on property rights—the most crucial of the "natural" individual rights which he is thought to have defended. The main points of his argument regarding the right of property in the state of nature may be summarized as follows:

Axiom: "God . . . . hath given the world to men *in common,* [and] hath also given them *reason* to make use of it."[7]

Axiom: "Men . . . . have a right to their preservation, and consequently to meat and drink and such other things as Nature affords for their subsistence."[8] This is merely a corollary of a proposition which he has put forward at an earlier point in the discussion: "The law of Nature . . . . willeth the peace and preservation of all mankind."[9]

With these two axioms (we call them axioms because Locke offers no "proof" for them except a Biblical reference which supports only the first[10]), he proceeds to explain that if this were the whole of the law of nature on the subject of property the purpose of the rule enunciated in the second axiom would in fact be defeated. The earth having been given to mankind in common, no one could "ever come to have a property in anything"[11] without an "express compact of all the commoners";[12] and "if such a consent as that was necessary, man had starved, notwith-

---

[5]ii. 7.
[6]ii. 11.
[7]v. 25 (italics mine).
[8]v. 24.
[9]ii. 7.
[10]*Psalms,* cxv. 16.
[11]v. 24.
[12]*Ibid.*

standing the plenty God had given him."[13] The difficulty may appear humorous in an age which, like ours, is unaccustomed to reasoning from first principles; but no one can read Locke's discussion of it without realizing that he took it very seriously indeed. Like the modern monetary heretic (whose position he anticipates by proposing a monetary explanation for the existence of poverty),[14] he sees mankind on the verge of annihilation, and nothing save his own (*i.e.*, Locke's) discovery to prevent disaster. Like the modern monetary heretic (in Mr. Keynes' phrase), he follows "with unbowed head wherever the argument leads him."[15] And his argument, proceeding as it does on two levels, is more ingenious by far than has been recognized by those who are responsible for current misapprehensions regarding his political theory.

On one level, Locke appears to take refuge in a "natural" right to property, which he deduces from a *third* axiom imported merely to provide a basis for such a deduction. "Every man," he writes, "has a 'property' in his own 'person.' This nobody has any right to but himself. The 'labour' of his body and the 'work' of his hands, we may say, are properly his."[16] From this it follows that nobody has a right to that with which a man has "mixed" his labor[17]—since in order to appropriate the mixture it would apparently be necessary to appropriate the labor which is one of its ingredients. If, therefore, a man mixes his labor with things (*e.g.*, apples, by picking them) which have hitherto been in the "common state," he must be regarded as having "removed" them from that common state, and as having thereby excluded the common right to them of other men.[18]

. . . . The turfs my servant has cut [!], and the ore I have digged in any place, where I have a right to them *in common* with others, become my property without the assignation or consent of anybody. The labour that was mine, removing them out of that common state they were in, hath fixed my property in them.[19]

Thus, apparently, if a man were to mix his labor with the entire food supply of his community, he would have fixed his property in it; and we should have the theory of property which is often attributed to John Locke—an *individualistic* theory akin to that which, according to Huntington Cairnes, has led English lawyers like Coke and Blackstone to regard property as a "natural right" superior to all other rights.[20] For, if

---

[13]v. 27. Query: Locke the originator of the notion of "starvation in the midst of plenty"?
[14]v. 36: "I dare boldly affirm, that the same rule of propriety—viz., that every man should have as much as he could make use of, would hold still in the world, *without straitening anybody*, ... had not the invention of *money* . . . . introduced (by consent) larger possessions" (italics mine).
[15]J. M. Keynes, *Treatise on Money* (London: Macmillan and Co., 1930), II, p. 216.
[16]v. 26.
[17]*Ibid.*
[18]v. 27.
[19]*Ibid.* (italics mine). Why not the servant's?
[20]Cf. Huntington Cairnes, *Law and the Social Sciences* (New York: Harcourt Brace and Co., 1935), pp. 65-79, for an illuminating discussion of the individualistic theory of property. Cf. Gierke, *op. cit.*, p. 108: "When Locke made personal liberty and property prior to all social organization, and treated these as the two inviolable rights which are entrusted by the individual to the State simply for protection, the ground-work was laid for a future theory of purely individualistic economics."

the product of a man's labor indeed be his, and if nobody ever have a right to it except himself, there can be no basis for a claim that his right to his property should on occasion be set aside for the convenience and welfare of others. And, if the theory be wrenched from context, and reproduced in a summary destined to appear in a history of political or economic theory, Locke can be construed as an ally of those who would make of security for property rights the foundation of society.

But, as is intimated above, the argument proceeds on a second level, and the theory we have just summarized is not Locke's theory at all. The right to acquire property by mixing one's labor with things held in common is not, in fact, put forward as a corollary of the right to one's person, but as a conclusion based upon *all three* of the axioms noticed above. This may be seen, in the first instance, from the fact that it applies *only* to things held in common. It may be seen, secondly, from the fact that Locke justifies it only as an *expedient*, dictated by that reason which God gave to mankind along with the earth, for preventing them from starving in the midst of plenty:

It is the taking any part of what is common, and removing it out of the state Nature leaves it in, which begins the property, *without which the common is of no use.*[21]

The right has its origin, then, in a need which Locke represents as a common (= community?) need.[22] And, thirdly, the dependence of his conclusion upon the first two axioms (for all its look of a deduction from the third axiom) is revealed in the fact that where Locke has to choose between the individual's right of property in that with which he has mixed his labor and the common right of men to their preservation, he unhesitatingly sacrifices the former to the latter:

The same law of Nature that does by this means give us property, does also bound that property too. . . . As much as any one can make use of to any advantage of life before it spoils, so much he may by his labour fix a property in. *Whatever is beyond this is more than his share, and belongs to others.*[23]

Indeed, in his discussion of property in land, Locke's language appears to commit him to the view that the burden is always upon the exerciser of the right of property to prove that "others" will not suffer from the appropriation; and the following lines make it abundantly clear that he is thinking of the right of property simply as a function of one's *duty* to enrich mankind's common heritage:

As much land as a man tills, plants, improves, cultivates, and can use the product of, so much is his property. . . . God, when He gave the world in common to all mankind, commanded man also to labour. . . . God and his reason commanded him to subdue the earth—*i.e.*, improve it for the benefit of life. . . . Nor was this

[21]v. 27 (italics mine). Cf. v. 29: "[The] law of reason makes the deer that Indian's who hath killed it."
[22]Cf. v. 36: "I have heard it affirmed that in Spain itself a man may be permitted to plough, sow, and reap, without being disturbed, upon land he has no other title to, but only his making use of it . . . . The inhabitants think themselves beholden to him who, by his industry . . . . has increased the stock of corn, which they wanted."
[23]v. 30 (italics mine).

appropriation of any parcel of land, by improving it, *any prejudice to any other man*. . . . He that leaves as much as another can make use of does as good as take nothing at all.[24]

We conclude that Locke's treatment of the right of property in the state of nature is predicated throughout upon assumptions which are collectivist in the extreme, and that he is in fact much closer to the *functional* view of property urged by modern critics of individualism[25] than to the natural rights view usually associated with his name. It is difficult, on this showing, to see how Professor Sabine can justify his unqualified statement that Locke set up, instead of the old theory of a natural law which enjoins the common good of a society, "a body of in- nate, indefeasible, individual rights which limit the competence of the community and stand as bars to prevent interference with the liberty and property of private persons."[26] For few modern defenders of a "public" right to interfere with the rights of property in the general in- terest have pressed the notion more vigorously than Locke did in such a passage as the following:

He that so employed his pains about any of the spontaneous products of Nature as any way to alter them from the state Nature put them in, by placing any of his labour on them, did thereby acquire a propriety in them; *but if they perished in his possession* . . . . *he offended against the common law of Nature,* and was liable to be punished: he invaded his neighbour's share, for he had no right farther than his use called for any of them, and they might serve to afford him con- veniencies of life.[27]

Furthermore, we may notice that this same *functional* view of rights carries itself over into Locke's handling of the problem of rights *in* or- ganized society. The right to withdraw from the state of nature and create an organized society is itself one which he tarries long enough to justify in terms of its effect upon others. "This [agreeing to join and unite into a community]," he explains, "any number of men may do, *be- cause it injures not the freedom of the rest*; they are left, as they were, in the liberty of the state of Nature."[28] This is unintelligible except on the hypothesis that he would have said, if pressed, that the right could *not* be exercised if it did injure the freedom of the rest—indeed, one of the great logical weaknesses of Locke's theory is that, having said so much, he fails to develop the notion of continuing responsibility on the part of his political community towards the world outside. However that may be, in discussing the situation which obtains within an organized com- monwealth, he represents rights always as created by that *law* which wills

[24]v. 31-32 (italics mine). Cf. v. 34: "Hence subduing or cultivating the earth and having dominion, we see, are joined together. *The one gave title to the other*" (italics mine).
[25]Cf. James Feibelman, *Positive Democracy* (Chapel Hill: University of North Carolina Press, 1940), p. 26: "The proper use of property would have to mean the adjustment of the property and of its owner to an established criterion of social function. Private property, then, is justified when by being private it furthers the common good."
[26]Sabine, *op. cit.*, p. 529.
[27]v. 37 (italics mine).
[28]viii. 95 (italics mine).

the good of the whole[29]—a point of view which emerges at its clearest in a neglected passage in which, speaking of the "right" to be represented in the commonwealth's legislative body, he argues that "no part of the people, however incorporated, can pretend to [it], *but in proportion to the assistance which it affords to the public.*"[30]

It remains to notice, in this connection, that Locke is in no sense open to the kind of criticism which Bradley and other collectivists have urged against those theorists who have represented social groups as artifacts pieced together by individuals.[31] According to Bradley, the individuals which such theories take as their point of departure nowhere exist; they are, just to the extent that they are conceived as being at any moment free from the influence of such groups, intellectual abstractions of the most vicious kind.[32] Bradley's attack upon the concept of the unsocialized individual is surely one of the most closely-reasoned demonstrations in recent philosophical literature, and bids fair to take its place, alongside of Butler's famous refutation of Hobbes, among those rare discussions which we may regard as—in Carritt's phrase—instances of "definite philosophical advance."[33] It is, therefore, significant that Locke's position is secure at every point from Bradley's line of attack. Not only does Locke call vigorous attention to the "dependency" of the child, through the early years of its existence, upon the assistance it receives from the social group known as the family (one of Bradley's major emphases),[34] not only is he deeply conscious (as was Bradley[35]) of the influence of the family and tradition in informing the child's mind[36] and determining his notions regarding right and wrong;[37] he also (like Bradley) stresses the relative helplessness of 'reformers against the inertia of the community's established institutions and customs.[38] Furthermore, Locke,

---

[29]ix. 130: "Being now in a new state . . . . he [man] is to part also with as much of his natural liberty . . . . as the good, prosperity, and safety of the *society* shall require" (italics mine).

[30]xiii. 158 (italics mine).

[31]Cf. Lamprecht, *op. cit.*, p. 131: "[Locke's] contract theory of the origin of civil society is not quite as individualistic in its implications as is Hobbes's; for he insisted that many social institutions have a natural origin in the pre-political state. Yet he certainly tended dangerously near to an atomic view of society." Cf. Aaron, *op. cit.*, p. 287: "[Locke's] individual is artificial. He has no family ties. He tends to be conceived as a somewhat isolated being even when he enters into social relations. So also Locke's state is artificial. It is a community of free and independent individuals bound together . . . . for the better security of their lives and estates—and it is nothing more."

[32]F. H. Bradley, *Ethical Studies* (London: Henry S. King & Co., 1876), p. 158: "The mere individual is a delusion of theory; and the attempt to realize it in practice is the starvation and mutilation of human nature, with total sterility or the production of monstrosities." Bradley summarizes the view he is criticizing as follows (*ibid.*, p. 148): "The family, society, the state, and generally every community of men, consists of individuals, and there is nothing in them real except the individuals. Individuals have made them and make them, by placing themselves and by standing in certain relations." Cf. G. D. H. Cole, *Social Theory* (London: Methuen & Co., 1920), p. 1: "Men do not make communities: they are born and bred into them."

[33]Carritt, *op. cit.*, p. 35.

[34]Bradley, *op. cit.*, p. 153. Cf. Locke, vii. 80; vi. 56.

[35]Bradley, *op. cit.*, p. 156.

[36]vi. 58. Cf. John Locke, *Essay Concerning Human Understanding* (Oxford: University Press, 1894), i. 2. 22.

[37]vi. 59.

[38]Bradley, *op. cit.*, pp. 182-183. Cf. xix. 223: "People are not so easily got out of their old forms as some are apt to suggest. They are hardly to be prevailed with to amend the acknowledged faults in the frame they have been accustomed to."

unlike Rousseau in his more mature thought, insists upon depicting even the state of nature as a community, and the law of nature as the law of a community.[39] Locke's individual is, we repeat, wherever you find him, a *community-member* by virtue of his participation, with other members of the community, in a common standard of justice; and any reference to Locke as an individualist must be read against the background of this phase of his thought.

The above argument must not be construed as meaning that Locke did not say things which appear to identify him with the doctrine of inherent natural rights. The position is, rather, that both the major emphases of his political theory and his concrete proposals with respect to governmental organization are inconsistent with that doctrine, and that the very sections of the *Second Treatise* in which that doctrine is enunciated embody a second doctrine which is not open to that objection. The existence of that second doctrine has seemed worth establishing even at the cost of the extremely lengthy discussion which has proved necessary for the purpose.

---

[39]ix. 128: " . . . . by which law, common to them all, he and all the rest of mankind are one community, make up one society distinct from all other creatures." Cf. Rousseau, *op. cit.*, i. 8.

CHAPTER V

THE LAW OF NATURE

As HAS BEEN intimated above, the argument of the present treatise is predicated upon the assumption that Locke's state of nature is an expository device,[1] and that he is not to be taken seriously when he pretends that it is a historical fact.[2] When, therefore, he explains that it is in order "to understand political power aright, and derive it from its original," that he proposes to describe "what estate all men are naturally in,"[3] we read him *as if he had said*:

Here we have certain commonwealths[4] which in fact exercise this right of making laws with penalties of death which I have defined as political power.[5] If we are to say what persons in such commonwealths ought to have political power, and how such things as commonwealths ever came to be created,[6] wouldn't it be a useful first step to visualize for ourselves the situation in which members of existing political societies *would find themselves* if their present governmental arrangements were abolished and their political societies dissolved?[7] What would their situation be? If we can answer that question, we should be able, by comparing that situation with the situations with which we are familiar, to decide whether or not it is right that political societies should exist, whether or not men should obey their commands, and whether some sets of arrangements are better than others—and if so, what criterion we may employ in order to distinguish good sets of arrangements from bad ones.

The device is one that the discipline of political theory could not well do without; and, had Locke used it well, students of that discipline would owe him a considerable debt of gratitude. But instead of using it well, he proceeded simply to lose himself in an argument whose complexity can be explained only on the hypothesis that he never really made up his mind what he was trying to prove with it. In the following paragraphs an attempt is made to break down that argument into some of its constituent theses, and (where that is possible) to suggest where, logically, each of them should have led him. All of them, it will be noticed, are develop-

---

[1] Cf. G. E. G. Catlin, *Principles of Politics* (New York: The Macmillan Co., 1930), p. 167: "It is irrelevant to enter into a full discussion of how far the theorists of social contract ever thought of the contract as having taken place at any historical epoch. A study of these writers would seem to lead to the conclusion that, although not uninfluenced by churchly discussions of what Adam did and classical discussions of the Golden Age which had once been, they were never guilty of this *naïveté.*"

[2] As he does on occasion. Cf. viii. 101: "If we may not suppose men ever to have been in the state of Nature, because we hear not much [!] of them in such a state, we may as well suppose the armies of Salmanasser or Xerxes were never children, because we hear little of them till they were men and embodied in armies . . . . Those [records] that we have of the beginning of any polities in the world . . . . are all either plain instances of such a beginning as I have mentioned, or at least have manifest footsteps of it." Cf. viii. 116, where he soberly refers to "unconfined inhabitants that run loose [in the woods]."

[3] ii. 4.

[4] Cf. ii. 9, where he names England, France, and Holland as "commonwealths."

[5] i. 3.

[6] i. 1.

[7] Pollock, *op. cit.*, p. 241: "This state [of nature] . . . . is rather a perfectly conscious abstraction than an attempt to construct the actual origin of society . . . . *The question is what a man's rights would be in the absence of positive institutions* . . . . The problem is not to account for the existence of society, but to ascertain its best or normal mode of existence" (italics mine).

ments of his major premise that, in the absence of government, men would still have duties towards one another (and, conversely, rights, since wherever there are duties there are rights to the performance of those duties), and that these duties and rights are enjoined by what he calls variously the law of God, the law of reason, and the law of nature.[8] While (*e.g.*) Brierly's argument for the necessity of postulating the existence of such a law[9] (thus for the validity of this phase of Locke's thought) appears to the present writer unanswerable, the present chapter will avoid that question and concern itself only with Locke's confusions regarding the *content* and *character* of such a law. To some extent the discussion will necessarily parallel that of preceding chapters.

Locke's theses regarding the law of nature are taken up at this point because they are indispensable for an evaluation of the insistence (central to his political theory) that, in the commonwealth (= state) as he describes it there is an *absolute* obligation on the part of the individual citizen to obey the law. We shall, that is to say, find Locke arguing that such a commonwealth has an *absolute right* to control the actions of its individual citizens and to dispose of their property—and, having once committed himself to a law of nature which embodies standards of right and wrong, he is clearly under an obligation to show that such an absolute right is not inconsistent with that law. If he ascribed several mutually incompatible contents to the law of nature (as the present chapter seeks to demonstrate), some of these must conflict with his later argument. But we can decide which theses do and which do not conflict with it only in the light of a previous understanding of the theses themselves.

First Thesis. The law of nature commands the "preservation" of *each* man—*i.e.*, of *each* man's life, liberty, and estate.

It is this one of Locke's theses regarding the law of nature that has given rise to the impression (which we have discussed above) that he moved in his thinking from the axiom that men have inalienable natural rights.[10] For, if one be prepared to reduce the supreme law to the proposition that the life, liberty, and estate of every person are sacred and inviolable, one must be prepared to defend the inevitable corollary that every person has an inalienable right to life, an inalienable right to liberty, and an inalienable right to property, thus inalienable rights—even if, like Locke, oneself has not chosen to use that particular form of words. Furthermore, if each person has under the supreme law a right to life, liberty, and estate, and if the supreme law be conceived as enjoining a duty upon each person to respect the rights it confers, then it is a short

[8]Cf. Lamprecht, *op. cit.*, pp. 81, 88.
[9]Cf. J. L. Brierly, *The Law of Nations* (Oxford: Clarendon Press, 1936), pp. 10-11: "Under a terminology which has ceased to be familiar to us the phrase [*i.e.*, law of nature] stands for something which no progressive system of law either does or can discard." Cf. *ibid.*, pp. 16-17.
[10]Cf. Wilson, *op. cit.*, p. 120.

step to the position that each person has (along with a duty to *respect* the rights of *others*) a duty to preserve his *own* life, liberty, and estate— *i.e.*, to Hobbes' belief that "justice therefore, ... is a rule of reason, by which we are forbidden to do anything destructive to our life; and consequently a law of Nature."[11] Locke does not—be it said to his credit—go quite that far; he chooses rather to speak of a right of self-preservation than of a duty when he must put a name to that which he has in mind;[12] but since he proceeds to treat it as if it were a duty, his disagreement with Hobbes and Rousseau[13] and other (more or less consistent) ethical hedonists appears to be largely verbal. Thus Locke's law of nature forbids suicide[14] (save for those who have "forfeited" their lives by committing certain crimes which deserve death[15]) ; and from the prohibition against suicide he is able to deduce a further prohibition against a man's subjecting himself to the "uncertain, unknown, arbitrary will of another man"[16]—surely not because he has a "right" to live and to be free? Furthermore, as we have already found him saying, "no *rational* creature [and for Locke the law of nature and the law of reason are the same thing] can be supposed to change his condition [= do anything at all?] with an intention to be worse."[17] The law of nature is, in short, a law which commands its subjects to look well to their own interests.

The proposition that the law of nature wills the preservation of each man must be sharply distinguished from the proposition (which we discuss below) that the law of nature wills the preservation of all mankind, for all that the former has the appearance of a logical deduction from the latter. Given a situation in which each man's life, liberty, and estate *can* be preserved without prejudice to the preservation of the life, liberty, and estate of any other, the two would perhaps come to the same thing; but Locke knew that by no means all situations are of that kind, and in his moments of greatest candor[18] (for he would certainly have liked to pass off the two propositions as identical) he makes the law of nature command that *mankind* be preserved "as much as possible."[19]

For our purposes, the most interesting of the passages in which he enunciates this (first) thesis is that in which he says, "Every one . . . .

---

[11]Hobbes, *Leviathan*, i. 15.

[12]ii. 11. Cf. vii. 87, where he speaks not of a "right" but of a "power." Cf. ii. 6: "Every one . . . . is bound to preserve himself."

[13]Cf. Rousseau, *op. cit.*, i. 2: "[La] première loi [de la nature de l'homme] est de veiller à sa propre conservation, ses premiers soins sont ceux qu'il se doit à lui-même." Cf. Carritt, *op. cit.*, p. 79 n.: "It is true that Locke was tarred with the same brush of psychological hedonism as Rousseau."

[14]iv. 22.

[15]*Ibid.*

[16]iv. 21.

[17]ix. 131 (italics mine).

[18]Waiving the extravagant possibility that Locke was unable to recognize incompatible propositions when they were set down in black and white before his eyes, it is difficult to avoid the suspicion that he is deliberately putting upon (*e.g.*) admirers of Hobbes when he writes (v. 24): "Natural reason . . . . tells us that *men*, being once born, have a right to their preservation" (italics mine). He proceeds at once to link "men" in the reader's mind with "mankind"; and the transition from each man's right to self-preservation to mankind's right to self-preservation is accomplished. This will not do.

[19]iii. 16.

when his own preservation comes not in competition, ought [= has a duty?] . . . . as much as he can to preserve the rest of mankind";[20] for here he faces the dilemma directly, and clearly chooses in favor of a law of nature which prefers the preservation of each to the preservation of "all."

Fidelity to this account of the law of nature would have committed Locke to the construction of a political society erected upon a *droit d'émigration* similar to that which figures in Rousseau's political system,[21] and/or rich in protective devices, like the United States Supreme Court, of which the individual might take advantage in husbanding his rights. For under this law of nature, the men in the state of nature would, before entering society, be obliged to demand assurances that they would never be asked to subordinate their own rights to those of other persons; and in the absence of such assurances they could not rightly avail themselves of the apparent advantages of life in organized society.

Second Thesis. The law of nature commands the preservation of all mankind—*i.e.,* the "good" of humanity.

It is this thesis about the law of nature which has been ignored by those writers who have regarded Locke as an extreme individualist. Since its presence in the *Second Treatise* has been amply established in our discussion of the (inconsistent) thesis that the law of nature wills the preservation of *each* man, we shall content ourselves with the citation of only one additional passage in which it is urged:

In transgressing the law of Nature, the offender declares himself to live by another rule than that of reason and common equity, which is that measure God has set to the actions of men for their mutual security, and so he becomes dangerous to mankind; the tie which is to secure them from injury and violence being slighted and broken by him, which *being a trespass against the whole species,* and the peace and safety of it, provided for by the law of Nature, every man upon this score, by the *right* he hath to preserve mankind in general, ... may bring such evil on any one who hath transgressed that law, as may make him repent . . . . and thereby deter him, and . . . . others from doing the like mischief.[22]

The passage is by no means free from the kind of mystification to which we have already directed the reader's attention—*i.e.,* Locke speaks of a "right" to preserve mankind, although (since the law of nature *provides* for the "peace and safety" of the "whole species") one would have expected the (unequivocal but hateful to Hobbesians) word "duty"; but it is the most unambiguous statement that Locke brought himself to make on the subject. It abounds with interesting implications. For one thing, it commits him definitely to the notion of a good which is (as we have anticipated in our own phrasing of the present thesis) that of a group, or collectivity (the "whole species"), rather than of persons viewed as

---

[20]ii. 6 (italics mine). Cf. vi. 57: "Law, in its true notion, is not so much the limitation as the direction of a free and intelligent agent to his proper interest."
[21]See below, p. 89.
[22]ii. 8 (italics mine).

individuals—a *general* as opposed to a *common* good. That group, Locke is saying here, is such by virtue of a *law* which acts as a "tie" between its members, and this law is a good belonging to the members in their collective (*i.e.,* not their individual) capacity, in the sense that it may not be broken by one of the members merely because he has ceased to regard it as *his* good. And when one of the members breaks the law which wills the good of the group, it is right that he should be punished, killed even, because the good of the members of the group "in general" (thus not necessarily all) should be preserved. In the second place, the passage acquits Locke of the suspicion, which certainly attaches to the other passages which we have brought forward in this connection, of having conceived the "preservation" of mankind in eudaemonist terms. It is, in part, security from "injury and violence," and deliverance from things which are noxious; but it involves also "reason and common equity," *i.e.,* justice.[23]

Here, then, is a law of nature which, by implication, commands (at most) as much of life, liberty, and estate for any particular man as is compatible with what we may (without violence to Locke's thought) call the interests of humanity (present and future, since it would "deter . . . . others from doing like mischief") in general, as defined by reason and equity. It is a law of nature which emphasizes the claims upon the individual of the broader interests of his fellow men, living and unborn, and, despite Locke's sleight-of-hand with the word "right," one which fixes attention upon the individual's *duty* to satisfy those claims.[24] It is a law of nature which involves no inalienable right for any man except the right to perform his duties and to be treated as a man (*i.e.,* as a "member" of mankind) so long (but only so long) as he does perform his duties. It is a law of nature which could enjoin an absolute duty to obey the law of a political society only where absolute obedience could be justified in terms of the individual's duties to his fellow men.

It is, nevertheless, absolute obedience to the law of a political society that we shall find Locke demanding; and he reveals, in the strictly political portions of the *Second Treatise,* no awareness whatever of any possible conflict between humanity's claims on the individual and the commonwealth's claims on the individual. Thus one of the hidden premises of his position is the notion that the "public good" of one's society is indistinguishable from the welfare of mankind. The duty enjoined by the present thesis becomes, therefore, a duty to promote the public good of one's society, as Locke moves from his discussion of the state of nature into his discussion of the commonwealth; and nothing more is said of the former duty.

---

[23]Cf. iii. 16: "When all cannot be preserved, the safety of the innocent is to be preferred."
[24]Wherefore he may be punished when he fails to satisfy them.

Third Thesis. The law of nature is a body of *immutable* rules regarding whose content no two rational men could disagree.

Locke does not, indeed, offer a list of such rules ("it would be beside my present purpose"[25]) ; but he does say definitely that the law of nature consists of "particulars"[26] which (as we have seen) are perhaps "plainer" than "the positive laws of commonwealths,"[27] and that "the municipal laws of countries" are "right" only to the extent that they are "founded on" (= consistent with?) those particulars.[28]

This is what Morris Cohen calls the "absolutistic conception of moral rules,"[29] and, despite its patent inconsistency with other attitudes expressed in the *Second Treatise,* its appeal to Locke's mind is revealed at many points in his argument. He believes, for example, that the "honour" which children owe to their parents is an obligation from which "no state, no freedom" can absolve them,[30] and that even the rule determining the age at which they are released from obedience to their parents "holds in all the laws a man is under, whether natural or civil."[31] He makes a similar claim for the rule which entitles injured persons to reparation for damages; civil authorities "can often, where the public good demands not the execution of the law, remit the punishment of criminal offences . . . . but yet *cannot remit the satisfaction due to any private man for the damage he has received*";[32] and for still other rules which he has occasion to cite in the course of his argument. The state of mind underlying such claims is too familiar to require elaboration;[33] it is the state of mind which enabled Calvin Coolidge to dismiss the problem of the war debts with the phrase, "Well, they hired the money, didn't they?"—a state of mind which, in politics, issues in the demand for "rigid" constitutions and the insistence that there are "principles" of jurisprudence to which laws must conform if they are to be accounted laws.

Far from being inconsistent with our first and second theses, the notion that the law of nature is reducible to unchangeable rules can keep house quite comfortably with either. It has been isolated for separate treatment here because it must be sharply distinguished from the fourth thesis, despite the fact that, like the fourth, it conduces logically to the view (sometimes attributed to the hierarchy of the Roman Catholic church) that any form of government is satisfactory which results in the enforcement of "good" laws.[34] Both the third and fourth theses, that is

---

[25]ii. 12.
[26]*Ibid.*
[27]See above, p. 64.
[28]ii. 12. Cf. xi. 135: "The obligations of the law of Nature cease not in society, but only in many cases are drawn closer, and have, by human laws, known penalties annexed to them."
[29]Cohen, *op. cit.,* p. 433.
[30]vi. 66.
[31]vi. 59.
[32]ii. 11 (italics mine). See above, p. 69.
[33]Cf. Cohen, *op. cit.,* p. 430: "Moral rules are most often viewed as absolute. It does not occur to most people that there *can* be genuine doubt about them."
[34]See above, p. 46.

to say, as, also, the first and second, are difficult to reconcile with the idea of any "right" of a political character except the right to enforce good laws.

Fourth Thesis. The law of nature is a law of "changing content" and thus commands different things in different objective situations.

The man who believes this can (as the man who believes our third thesis evidently cannot) make his peace with the notion that men's rights (and duties) are capable of definition only in terms of the context in which they are to be exercised (and performed). The attempt to reduce right to immutable rules is, therefore, likely to appeal to such a man as resting upon a fundamental misapprehension regarding the nature of right, which, whether it command the preservation of each man or that of the whole species, enjoins that line of conduct which in a given situation will in fact minister to the realization of the end in question. He is not committed to a denial that there are rules which, over a long period of time and in a wide variety of situations, have proved capable of such ministration—rules with regard to which there is, in all situations, a powerful presumption that they ought to be obeyed. But he cannot conceive of a moral rule which is absolute, and cannot understand how the exponent of our third thesis can have convinced himself (as, *e.g.*, Kant succeeded in doing with respect to lying) that rules should be obeyed even when obedience will militate against the purpose upon which they depend for their validity. Carried out to its ultimate implications, in one direction, it leads to our sixth thesis and thus to the politics of the philosophical anarchist—*i.e.*, to the position that the individual, who alone can have an adequate knowledge of his situation, must make his own rules from moment to moment. Carried out to its ultimate implications in another direction it leads (as we have observed above) to an insistence that positive law can claim binding character only where it commands that which *in the existing situation* is right—and, conversely, that positive law which does command that which is right ought to be obeyed no matter what is the character of the government which commands it.

It is not, as it happens, possible to point to many passages in the *Second Treatise* in which Locke enunciated this doctrine, and there appears to be no doubt that, of the two, our *third* thesis was by far the more congenial to his manner of thinking—as, also, there appears to be no doubt that our fifth thesis was more attractive to him than either the third or the fourth. Nevertheless, the fourth thesis is clearly presupposed in (*e.g.*) the reasoning by which he seeks to explain the fact that, in countries *"where there are plenty of people under government who have money and commerce,"* a man is *not* free, as we have seen him to be in other conditions, to appropriate such common land as he can make use of. "The remainder," Locke says,

. . . . would not be as good to the rest of the commoners as the whole was . . . . whereas in the beginning . . . . of the world it was quite otherwise. *The law man was under was rather for appropriating* . . . . God, by commanding to subdue, gave authority so far to appropriate. And *the condition of human life, which requires labour and materials to work on, necessarily introduce* [*sic*] *private possessions.*[35]

And it reveals itself once more in what he says (despite the fact that a readily intelligible "law of Nature stands as an eternal rule to all men, legislators as well as others")[36] regarding the need for promptly assembling the legislature of his commonwealth when "the quick turn of affairs [is] . . . . such as to need their present help":[37]

Any delay of their convening might endanger the public; and sometimes . . . . the limited time of their sitting might be too short for their work, and rob the public of that benefit which could be had only from their mature deliberation.[38]

Fifth Thesis. The law of nature, in its application to any aggregate of persons, may be "amended" by agreement (explicit or tacit) among those persons; and the rules resulting from such agreements have the binding force of the law of nature itself. We say "aggregate" rather than "group" because fidelity to Locke's thought on this point demands a word which fixes attention upon the fact that the persons in question do not, in order to take advantage of this *carte blanche* regarding the content of the law of nature, need any organizational arrangements beyond those necessary for making such an agreement. "Keeping of faith," he writes, "belongs to men as men, and not as members of society."[39]

The effect of such a doctrine is, clearly, to reduce the law of nature—as nearly as possible—to the rule *pacta sunt servanda.* The law of nature imposes duties and confers rights (whether for the good of each or for the good of the species). B has a duty to respect A's rights, and A has a right to the performance of that duty by B, and *vice versa*; but if A and B wish to agree to a different complex of rights and duties *as between themselves,* it is, once the agreement is concluded, the new complex which they must observe. In short, the law of nature bids me, above all else, to keep my word.

That such a doctrine can be pressed only at the cost of calling into question the validity of the first, second, third, and fourth theses, is too obvious to require comment. If I am to keep a promise which proves to involve loss of my life, liberty, or estate, what becomes of that law of nature which commands me to look well to my own preservation? If I am to perform my contract, even when performance would militate

---

[35]v. 34 (italics mine).
[36]xi. 135.
[37]xiii. 156.
[38]*Ibid.* Cf. *ibid.*: "Constant, frequent meetings of the legislative, and long continuations of their assemblies, without necessary occasion, could not but be burdensome to the people."
[39]ii. 14. Wherefore "the promises . . . . between a Swiss and an Indian, in the woods of America, are binding to them."

against the interest of the species, what becomes of that law of nature which wills the preservation of all mankind?[40] If rules may be changed by agreement (thus also by an agreement which even a reasonable man could not have been expected to anticipate) what becomes of the doctrine that the law of nature consists of universally valid particulars plain to any "studier" of that law? And if promises are to be fulfilled, at whatever cost, what becomes of the thesis that rights and duties vary with circumstances?

We must, to be sure, restrain any impulse to be over-severe in taxing Locke with this inconsistency, for the problem involved is one of the most difficult which has arisen in the history of ethical speculation. Every moralist believes that, other things being equal, a man ought to keep his promises. But every moralist (including Locke himself) believes that a man has other duties besides that of keeping promises, and that he ought to perform these duties as well; and the interesting problems begin where there is a conflict between a man's duty to keep his promise and some other duty whose performance is clearly incumbent upon him. The thing for which we *may* properly chide Locke is his failure to notice the possibility of such a conflict; and it is (in the opinion of the present writer) hardly too much to say that the strategy of the *Second Treatise* consists precisely in a persistent refusal to recognize the fact that, at the limit, a man may not be able to obey the law of nature as described in this fifth thesis *and* the law of nature as described in the first and the second theses, and that, at the limit, a similar difficulty arises as between (*e.g.*) the first and the second, the third and the fourth, and the fifth and the sixth theses. By no means the least of the virtues of the *Contrat social* (as compared with the *Second Treatise*) lies in the fact that its author, deeply indebted as he was to Locke,[41] appears to have written in full awareness of this difficulty in his thought.

The present thesis bears a family resemblance to, but must not be confused with, our sixth thesis below. This resemblance may be seen most readily when, for the form of words which we have employed at the beginning of our discussion of the fifth thesis, we substitute the equivalent proposition "a man can be bound by his own consent," and choose, from among the various ways of stating the sixth thesis, that which affirms that "nothing is binding upon a man except that to which he *consents*." That the resemblance is, however, only superficial, emerges very clearly indeed when we pause to consider the implications of the two

---

[40]Which is not to deny that there is, up to a point, a general interest in the keeping of promises and the performance of contracts. But there appears to be no simple answer to the question, Up to what point?

[41]Cf. Jean-Jacques Rousseau, *Lettres de la montagne* (Paris: P. Dupont, 1823), p. 348: "Locke, Montesquieu, l'abbé de Saint-Pierre, ont traité les mêmes matières et souvent avec la même liberté tout au moins. *Locke en particulier les a traitées exactement dans les mêmes principes que moi*" (italics mine). Cf. T. H. Green, *Lectures on the Principles of Political Obligation* (London: Longmans, Green, and Co., 1917), p. 68: "The essential ideas of Rousseau are to be found in Locke's *Treatise of Civil Government.*"

propositions with respect to the special problems of politics—understanding by "politics" the logic of that coercive state whose apparent necessity we have discussed briefly in Chapter I. For, if a man must invariably keep his promises, the thing which matters most in any specific political situation is what he (and others) can be shown to *have* consented to; and if he (and the others) can be shown to have consented to obey (*e.g.*) all rules made in a certain way, we may properly demand of him, when the time comes at which he wishes that the consent had not been given or believes that it ought not to have been given, that he nevertheless obey until he can persuade all of those with whom he has covenanted that the agreement should be rescinded. It is quite otherwise if we think from the notion that nothing binds a man except that to which he *consents*; for here the thing that matters is not that to which he consented yesterday or the day before, but that to which he gives his willing approval today. The former notion conduces, logically, to the basic doctrines of modern constitutionalism; the latter to a denial that a coercive state (in the sense intended in our first chapter) can be squared with the fundamental principle of morality.

We have already noticed, in our discussion of Locke's theory of property, his argument to the effect that the natural law prohibition against a man's having more than he can make use of, could be set aside by a tacit agreement among men to "put a value on" money—which means, if it means anything at all, that the law of nature may be changed by unanimous agreement from a law which provides for economic distribution on the basis of need into a law which provides for economic distribution on the *sauve qui peut* basis of modern capitalism.[42] "It is plain," he says, "that the consent of men have [*sic*][43] agreed to a disproportionate and unequal possession of the earth."[44] He disposes, similarly, of the rule which makes of each man in the state of nature (= apart from agreements to the contrary) the executor of the law of nature,[45] as, also, of the rule which declares a man free (in the state of nature) to refuse his assistance, in any particular case, to those who propose to enforce observance of the law of nature upon a recalcitrant.[46] And, while he certainly speaks sometimes as though there were matters which cannot be dealt with in this way (*e.g.*, with regard to the rights and duties of parents and children),[47] and must speak in this way unless he is willing to abandon entirely our third thesis, our point here is that there are other times at which he makes no exceptions at all: "Whatever engagements

[42]v. 36.
[43]We call attention to the fact that Locke may be using the word "consent" by analogy with *consensus* in post-Classical Latin, in which (*e.g.*) *consensus hominum* is often used as synonymous with *omnes*, and is therefore frequently construed with a plural verb.
[44]v. 50.
[45]ii. 7. Cf. vii. 89.
[46]ii. 10. Cf. vii. 88.
[47]vi. 52-76.

or promises any one made for himself, he is under the obligation of them."[48] According to the fifth thesis in its purest form, therefore, men have an unlimited competence to modify the law of nature by agreement, and an unlimited obligation to obey the law in its amended form until it is changed again by unanimous agreement.

It seems probable, however, that for a clear understanding of what Locke intended his doctrine of consent to mean we must read it against the background of (1) his insistence that a man's consent can, although it may be given tacitly, be given by himself alone—*i.e.*, not by someone else for him,[49] (2) that the consent, whether express or tacit, must be given freely and not under duress,[50] and (3) that there is *one* sort of agreement to which a man may not consent at all. Because it involved him in a difficulty from which he never succeeded in escaping (and one of which we shall say much in what follows), it is the third of these qualifications of the doctrine which is, for our purposes, the most important; and before proceeding to our sixth thesis it will be well for us to examine it carefully.

The kind of agreement which Locke wishes to prohibit is, briefly, one which results in the *complete* subjection of one man's will to the will of another man, or of other men. Like Krabbe in our own time, and like (in the opinion of the present writer) all of the majority-rule democrats, Locke moves in his thought from a horror of *personal* authority; and one of the surest bits of evidence to which we may point, in substantiation of the suggestion that students of politics have got out of the habit of reading Locke, is the fact that the central notion of the following eloquent lines suggests to our minds not the name of the author of the *Second Treatise* but rather that of Lord Acton: "He that thinks absolute power purifies men's blood, and corrects the baseness of human nature, need but read the history of this, or any other age, to be convinced to the contrary."[51] To give one man absolute power over another (or over others) is, he thinks, to invite the former to violate that provision of the law of nature which forbids men to treat one another "as if we were made for one another's uses";[52] and to suppose that men ever willingly agree to the exercise of such power over themselves is "to think [them] . . . . so foolish that they take care to avoid what mischiefs may be done them by polecats or foxes, but are content, nay, think it safety, to be devoured

---

[48]viii. 116.
[49]viii. 119: "Every man [is] . . . . naturally free, and nothing [is] . . . . able to put him into subjection to any earthly power, but only his own consent." Thus, a man "cannot by any compact whatsoever bind his children or posterity" (viii. 116).
[50]xvi. 186: "It remains only to be considered whether promises, extorted by force, without right, can be thought consent, and how far they bind. To which I shall say, they bind not at all; because whatsoever another gets from me by force, I still retain the right of, and he is obliged presently to restore."
[51]vii. 92. Cf. Dalberg-Acton, *op. cit.*, pp. 48-49. Cf. xvi. 180: "The practice of the strong and powerful, how universal soever it may be, is seldom the rule of right."
[52]ii. 6.

by lions."[53] "I have reason," he insists elsewhere, "to conclude that he who would get me into his power . . . . would use me as he pleased when he had got me there, and destroy me too when he had a fancy to it; for nobody can desire to have me in his absolute power unless it be to . . . . *make me a slave*."[54] To agree to become a slave (in this sense) is, for Locke, tantamount to agreeing to one's own death; and he insists (a) that no man in his senses can be supposed to do either willingly, and (b) that even if a man were willing to do one of them, the agreement would be invalid because in violation of the law of nature: "A man, not having the power of his own life, cannot by compact or his own consent enslave himself to any one, nor [sic] put himself under the absolute, arbitrary power of another . . . . Nobody can give more power than he has himself."[55]

What this fifth thesis (taken with its qualifications) amounts to, then, is this: I must keep my promises—but a promise is not a promise if made under duress, if made for me by someone else, or if it subjects my will to the absolute, arbitrary authority of a will not my own. Evidently a theorist who, like Holland, is unable to conceive of political authority as other than personal, would have to interpret such a thesis as meaning that a man can subject himself to no coercive authority at all—since, on his showing, such authority always turns out (when the time comes for it to be exercised) to be that of the persons responsible (in the particular instance) for its being set in motion. But it is of the first importance that exegesis of the *Second Treatise* should proceed from a clear understanding that Locke did *not* interpret it in this manner, and that he *was* able to conceive of an authority to whose compulsion men might freely subject themselves without becoming slaves in the sense intended in the excerpt reproduced above—*i.e.*, the impersonal authority of the Law. Indeed, not the least of the injustices of which Krabbe is guilty, in his over-hasty summary of previous speculation on the problem with which he deals in *Die moderne Staats-idee*, lies in his failure to recognize in Locke the elements of his own theory of the sovereignty of law. In his discussion of Rousseau he writes:

Mit dieser Vorstellung von einer als Person organisierten und wirkenden Gemeinschaft, welche Macht über ihre Glieder besitzt, ist ein neuer und fruchtbarer Gedanke in der Staatslehre in den Vordergrund getreten, weil damit zum ersten Male die Autorität einer unpersönlichen Gewalt gesetzt wird. Bis auf Rousseau kann mann sich keine andere als eine persönliche Gewalt denken, und wird in der Staatsmacht ein bestimmten Personen zustehender Befehlsrecht gesehen.[56]

And in his discussion of Locke's theory:

Der Zusammenhang zwischen Staat und Gemeinschaft liegt also nur hierin, dass der erstere eine notwendige Ergänzung der zweiten ist, nicht aber dass die Obrig-

[53] vii. 93.
[54] iii. 17 (italics mine).
[55] iv. 22.
[56] Krabbe, *op. cit.*, pp. 30-31.

keitsgewalt ein Bestandteil der aus der Gemeinschaft hervorgekommenen Rechts-
ordnung ist und also die nämliche Grundlage hat wie das in der Gemeinschaft
herrschende Recht.[57]

Many years before Rousseau posited *zum ersten Male* the authority of
impersonal power, Locke had written of the "sovereign" (= king) in
his system:

[He] is to be considered as the image, phantom, or representative of the commonwealth, acted by the will of the society declared in its laws, and thus he has no
will, no power, but that of the law. . . . When he quits this representation, this
public will, and acts by his own private will, he . . . . is but a single private person
without power and without will; *the members owing no obedience but to the public
will of the society.*[58]

If Krabbe had meant merely that Locke, having proclaimed the sovereignty of law, proceeded to argue for the legitimacy of a state whose
citizens may at any moment find themselves subject to the absolute,
arbitrary will of other persons, he might be credited with the discovery
of the major difficulty in Locke's position. Locke's capital error, that is
to say, is that of denying in one portion of his argument the ethical
defensibility of the kind of society for which he pleads in another—of
saying here that obedience is owed *only* to the Law (= that which the
law ought to be), and there that one should obey a state whose law is,
at the limit, merely the command of certain persons. Krabbe could, however, hardly have isolated this error in Locke's position without recog-
nizing it in his own—without, further, perceiving (as Rousseau did) that
the attempt to set up an authority which is both impersonal *and* authori-
tative is a circle-squaring expedition, for failure in which no man is to be
censured.[59]

Sixth Thesis. The law of nature commands that, at the limit, each
man shall act in accordance with the dictates of his own reason.

This is by much the most elusive of Locke's six theses regarding the
content of the law of nature—as, because of the rôle it was destined to
play in Rousseau's political system, it is the most interesting. Stated in
its very simplest terms, it becomes an insistence that after all has been
said that can be said about right and wrong (= about the content of the
law of nature), after we have decided whether the end is the good of
the species or the good of each man, after we have decided whether right
can or cannot be reduced to rules, after we have decided to what extent
promises create a special sphere of right in which all rules are suspended

[57]*Ibid.*, p. 26.
[58]xiii. 151 (italics mine). Cf. xviii. 206: "The king's authority being given him only by the
law, he cannot empower any one to act against the law, or justify him by his commission in so
doing . . . . Against the laws there can be no authority." Cf. the following formula from
Laband (*ap.* Krabbe, *op. cit.*, p. 1), of which Krabbe makes much: "Der Staat von seinen
Angehörigen keine Leistung und keine Unterlassung fordern, ihnen nichts befehlen und nichts
verbieten kann, als auf Grund eines Rechtssatzes." The latter might well be a plagiarism from
Locke.
[59]Rousseau, *Gouvernement de Pologne*, p. 252: "Mettre la loi au-dessus de l'homme est un
problème en politique que je compare à celui de la quadrature du cercle en géométrie. Résolvez
bien ce problème; et le gouvernement fondé sur cette solution sera bon et sans abus. Mais
jusque-là soyez sûrs qu'où vous croirez faire régner les lois, ce seront les hommes qui régneront."

except *pacta sunt servanda,* there remains the problem, analogous to that of administration (as compared to legislation) in politics—namely, that of who is to make the decisions regarding the application of agreed standards to specific situations. Even if, for example, we were to place beyond challenge the rule *pacta sunt servanda,* opinions might well differ in a given case as to whether a promise has been given, as to the nature of the promise, as to whether non-performance by one party to an agreement excuses the second party from his obligation, as to whether such non-performance has been demonstrated, *etc.*[60] Some ethical philosophers, confronted with this problem, have taken the position that in the last analysis the individual's duty is to do his duty as *he* sees it—while others have emphasized the fallibility of the individual's reason and the resultant need for Authority capable of relieving the individual of all responsibility for such decisions. Carritt, for example, writes:

I think we must say that there are right acts for a rational being to perform [*i.e.*, that there is what Locke calls a law of reason], whether he knows what they all are or not, *but that we cannot blame him for not doing them if he cannot know them.*[61]

Locke, in detailing the terms of the compact which underlies his political society, says (approvingly):

All private judgment of every particular member being excluded, the community comes to be umpire, and by understanding indifferent rules and men authorised by the community for their execution, decides all the differences that may happen between any members of that society concerning any matter of right. . . . ; whereby it is easy to discern who are, and are not, in political society together.[62]

But Locke did not always use this language; and as a result there is a line of argument in the *Second Treatise,* closely related to that distrust of personal authority of which we have taken notice above, which amply justifies the inclusion here of this sixth thesis.

It is, he believes, good that men should establish an authority to decide differences between them regarding matters of right, and it is good that, having established such an authority, they should abide by its decrees. It must, however, be an authority under which they can count upon an "established, settled, known law,"[63] a "known and indifferent judge,"[64] and due execution of the latter's sentences[65]—an authority, in short. which meets at every point the familiar requirements of Dicey's "rule of law."[66] But, in any case, they retain

---

[60]With regard to the argument in the text that it was this (sixth) one of Locke's theses which most deeply influenced Rousseau, cf. Rousseau, *ap.* Charles William Hendel, *Jean-Jacques Rousseau: Moralist* (London: Oxford University Press, 1934), II, p. 176: "Since I feel myself bound to everything that I have either expressed or intended to express in my dealings, *I am not bound to anything whatsoever beyond that"* (italics mine). *I.e.*, Rousseau is to decide regarding the extent of his obligation.

[61]E. A. Carritt, *The Theory of Morals* (Oxford: Oxford University Press, 1928), p. 140 (italics mine).

[62]vii. 87.

[63]ix. 124.

[64]ix. 125.

[65]ix. 126.

[66]A. V. Dicey, *The Law of the Constitution* (London: Macmillan and Co., 1927), pp. 179-201.

that ultimate determination . . . . which belongs to all mankind, where there lies no appeal on earth, *by a law antecedent and paramount to all positive laws of men,* whether they have just cause to make their appeal to Heaven. And this judgment they cannot part with.[67]

To "make appeal to Heaven" is, be it noted, a euphemism which Locke employs where a modern writer would say "to fight it out"; and Locke's point is—at his most reckless—that

where the body of the people, *or any single man,* are deprived of their right, or are under the exercise of a power without right, having no appeal on earth they have a liberty to appeal to Heaven whenever *they* judge the cause of sufficient moment.[68]

The man who makes the appeal must, to be sure, remember that he will answer for it before a tribunal which is not dependent for its knowledge upon the evidence it hears, and one which will deal harshly with him if he has for frivolous reasons inconvenienced his fellow citizens;[69] he must, therefore, be sure not only that he is right but also that the issue at stake is "worth the trouble and cost of the appeal."[70] But if he *is* sure, he is entitled to make the appeal.

The contemporary student of politics should, in all this, feel himself on familiar ground, for it is this train of thought which constitutes the common element in the (otherwise not very homogeneous) works of Harold J. Laski; but its presence in the *Second Treatise* creates for its author yet another logical difficulty from which there is no escape. If, at the limit, it is really right for the individual to judge for himself whether or not he will permit force to be used on him, then, as Rousseau argued, the only legitimate political society is that which maintains an *effective* right of emigration and thus makes all of its decisions unanimously.[71] The implications of the sixth thesis are, that is to say, unavoidably anarchistic, and cannot be squared with those aspects of Locke's political thought which we are about to examine.

---

[67]xiv. 168 (italics mine). Cf. xiii. 155: "In all states and conditions the true remedy of force without authority is to oppose force to it." Cf. xix. 242: "Force between either persons who have no known superior on earth, or which permits no appeal to a judge on earth, [is] . . . . properly a state of war, wherein the appeal lies only to Heaven; and in that state the injured party must judge for himself when he will think fit to make use of that appeal and put himself upon it." Cf.: iii. 20; xix. 241; xix. 232, where he says that where one man uses force upon another without right "all former ties are cancelled, all other rights cease, and every one has a right to defend himself, and to resist the aggressor."

[68]xiv. 168 (italics mine).

[69]xvi. 176. Note that the right is thus made to defend itself in terms of the general interest.

[70]*Ibid.*

[71]Everything Rousseau had to say about majority-rule should be read with this in mind. By remaining within the society, the minority definitely associates itself with the majority's decision, which thus becomes unanimous. Cf. Rousseau, *Contrat social,* iv. 2: "Quand l'État est institué, le consentement est dans la résidence; habiter le territoire, c'est se soumettre à la souveraineté . . . . Ceci doit toujours s'entendre d'un État libre; car d'ailleurs la famille, les biens, le défaut d'asile, la nécessité, la violence, peuvent retenir un habitant dans le pays malgré lui, et alors son séjour seul ne suppose plus son consentement." Cf. Catlin, *Principles,* p. 388, n. 2: "Rousseau's entire argument for the claims of the State . . . . rests on the validity of this footnote . . . . [The] assumption . . . . is obviously fantastic . . . . Present-day States are not *états libres* in Rousseau's sense." Indeed they are not; and Catlin, having made the point himself, should not identify. Rousseau with the majority-rule democrats, who certainly are not thinking in terms of a *droit d'émigration.* Cf. Id., *Story of the Political Philosophers,* pp. 453-54, where his criticism of Rousseau reveals no awareness of this limitation upon the right of the majority in Rousseau's system. Here, as elsewhere, it is Locke who expresses the real views of the majority-rule democrats (viii. 121): "He that has once, by actual agreement . . . . given his consent to be of any commonweal, is perpetually and indispensably obliged to be, and remain unalterably a subject to it." Locke concedes a right of emigration to residents who have given *tacit* consent, but does not make the individual's obligation depend (as Rousseau does) on his being in a position to exercise it.

CHAPTER VI

POPULAR SOVEREIGNTY

SINCE Locke certainly claimed (in reply to his question regarding the "way of designing and knowing the persons that have" political power) for the majority of the members of his political society all the power which the society itself could rightfully exercise,[1] the validity of our thesis that he was an extreme majority-rule democrat is most likely to be questioned by those who regard his theory as one in which there is no room for the concept of sovereignty as we today understand it. Locke's majority, they may object, was to have its way only within certain carefully defined limits (*i.e.*, within the limits set by the natural rights which he attributes to the members of his society). If the majority (or the people) were to ignore these limits, it would find itself exercising powers which Locke denies to the society itself. Locke, in a word, could not possibly have countenanced the notion of an unlimited sovereignty, either in the whole people or in a majority of the people.

We have, as the reader will recall, taken the liberty of treating Locke's state of nature as an expository device, the purpose of which is to show what men's rights and duties would be in the absence of formal political organization. Proceeding on this assumption, we have attempted to analyze Locke's account of those rights and duties into irreducible first principles of ethics—always, however, emphasizing the fact that they are intended to apply to a situation in which, by definition, there is no political organization, and, wherever possible, calling attention to their mutual incompatibility.

We shall, in the same way, treat Locke's "compact" as an expository device, whose purpose is to lay bare the essential character of the rights and duties which belong to men as members of (legitimate) commonwealths.[2] That is, we shall proceed *as if Locke had said to the reader*:

A commonwealth, in my view, is simply a group of people occupying a given territory and, normally, obeying a common government. All of us are familiar with such groups of persons, and all of us are accustomed to distinguish in our minds between those situations in which the members of a commonwealth are under an obligation to obey their present government and those situations in which we are unable to perceive any such obligation. Or, if you like, physical power to promulgate and enforce laws sometimes, in this commonwealth or that

---

[1]See below, p. 112.
[2]Cf. J. Allen Smith, *The Growth and Decadence of Constitutional Government* (New York: Henry Holt & Co., 1930) pp. 167-168: "[Locke] did not contend that the social contract was the origin of all governments, but merely of all legitimate governments . . . . A fair interpretation of his political philosophy justifies the assumption that any part which the social contract may have had in the remote past in the creation of political institutions was, in his opinion, of minor importance in comparison with the significance of the social contract doctrine as a theory of political organization."

one, gets into the hands of persons who have no right to exercise it, and use it to enforce rules which ought not to be obeyed. Unfortunately, however, our ideas on this question are extremely indefinite, thus greatly in need of clarification; and the need is all the greater because two recent writers, Filmer and Hobbes, have said things about it which, at least in my own opinion, are iniquitous. I believe myself to have discovered certain principles which will serve, for those of us who disagree with Filmer and Hobbes, as reliable criteria by which to distinguish governments which ought to be obeyed from those which ought not.

Briefly, the way in which I have arrived at these principles is as follows. I start out by assuming that organization for purposes of government is a necessity for human beings—a notion which we may express either by saying (as I sometimes do in a metaphorical sense) that men were not willing when they were in the state of nature (= in an unorganized condition) to remain in it, or by saying (what comes to the same thing) that they would not willingly return to the state of nature even if they were free to do so.

At the same time, I assume that they are not so eager for the benefits of life in an organized political society as to be willing to pay an unlimited price for them. They desire certain conveniences which can be had only through organization, *i.e.*, certain rights, and are willing to accept certain burdens (which we shall call duties) in order to assure themselves those conveniences; but if the onerousness of the burdens were obviously disproportionate to the desirability of the conveniences, they would not be willing to accept the former—nor would it be fair, in that event, to expect them to do so.

I assume, thirdly, that it is possible to infer, from what we know about people, what *inconveniences* would weigh most heavily upon them in the absence of political organization; and that it is proper for us to posit the removal of those inconveniences as the *minimum* which they ought (if the exchange is to be a fair one) to receive from their political society in return for the acceptance of any burdens whatever. Those inconveniences are, pretty obviously, the absence of any commonly accepted law defining men's rights and duties, the lack of an impartial judge to decide disputes regarding matters of right, and, finally, the helplessness of the weak man with right on his side against the unjust man who happens to be strong.[3] We may, therefore, point to the following facilities which a political society must be able to offer to its members in return for the duties which it imposes upon them: promulgated, standing laws defining the rights and duties of all the members; arrangements for impartial decisions on matters of right; and unfailing protection of the members in the enjoyment of their rights.[4] A society which fails to provide these facilities is not really a political society at all, but a continuation of the state of nature. In other words, we shall regard men as organized only when they are organized in such a way as to be free of the inconveniences of the state of nature.

In the fourth place, having gone so far already as to speak in terms of a fair exchange between the society and its members, I assume that the most convenient method we can employ in describing the duties which the members must accept in order for the society to be able to provide the facilities set forth above is that of pretending that a contract has been negotiated between the members of the society, setting forth the burdens they are willing to shoulder in return for such facilities. In other words, I shall speak as if such a society could come into existence only by virtue of a promise given by each of its members to accept certain duties and faithfully discharge them—which is only another way of saying that such a society can continue to exist only if it can count on its members to act *as if* they were under contract for the performance of certain duties.

I propose in this book, then, to expound my views as to the nature of the promise which individuals must be understood to have given if their society is really to deliver them from the inconveniences of life outside society—*i.e.*, the

[3]ix. 124-126.
[4]ix. 131.

understandings which must exist between the individuals in a society in order for the latter to be capable of achieving the purposes for which it exists.

The chief of these understandings which Locke demands of the citizens of his commonwealth are (1) an understanding with regard to the *purpose* for which the society's power is to be used; (2) an understanding as to the kind of obedience which each member of the society may expect the other members to tender to the society's law; and (3) an understanding as to the way in which the society's laws are to be made.

The most immediately interesting of these understandings, for our present purposes, is the first. If the reader will turn back to Locke's definition of political power[5] he will observe that it contains the words "and all this only for the public good." It is, as it stands, an apparent limitation upon the power of the society (*i.e.*, the power of the society cannot be employed *except* for the promotion of the public good)—and, at the same time, a grant of power to the society (*i.e.*, to take action for the public good). Whether or not it *is*, in the treatment it receives at Locke's hands, a limitation upon the society's power, is a question to which we shall return at a later point, our present concern being to direct attention to Locke's failure to give an adequate account of what he understood the phrase to mean. There is no *a priori* objection to the notion (already mentioned briefly in our discussion of Locke's law of nature) that men may become so related to one another in a collectivity as to justify us in speaking in terms of a good which is that of the collectivity rather than that of its members regarded as individuals. Nor is there any objection *a priori* to the notion that men may become so related to one another in a collectivity as to be willing to sacrifice their narrow interests as individuals to the broader interests of the collectivity. Much of the history of humankind would be incomprehensible but for the possibility of appealing to such an hypothesis, and the prospects for the future moral development of mankind would seem dismal indeed but for the possibility of indulging the hope that it is true. Nevertheless, to concede the utility of the concept is not to concede that it should be loosely used, and we cannot face too early, in our study of Locke, the fact that he was completely unaware of its presuppositions.[6] He should have seen (but did not) that if there is to be a good "public" to a group of individuals, they must have, over a considerable area, interests which are really common, and that, conversely, where such common interests do not exist, there is no point in speaking of a public good. Rousseau was well aware of these presuppositions, and uses the concept of the *"bien public"*

---

[5]See above, p. 66.
[6]Cf. Lamprecht, *op. cit.*, p. 135 n.: "Locke did not distinguish between the common good and the good of each separate person, but assumed always that the former included the latter. . . . . Locke does not give any indication of having realized that there is any problem in this identification of private and public interests."

with notable precision.[7] Locke lacks Rousseau's insight into the fact that, were the men in a commonwealth without recognized common interests, the maintenance of authority would be impossible, while if their interests did not conflict authority would be unnecessary, that, therefore, a sort of equilibrium between centrifugal and centripetal tendencies is a logical presupposition of political society.[8] When, therefore, what he wants to show is that government is necessary, he speaks as if men's interests were so divergent as to deprive the notion of a good common to them of all meaning; and when what he wants to show is that obedience pays good returns, he simply takes for granted the existence of enough common interests to constitute a public good—and without realizing that this makes his conclusions inapplicable to situations where that assumption is not fulfilled. If, that is to say, Locke had been really aware of the area of common interests whose existence is assumed in his concept of a public good, he would have contented himself with arguing (as Rousseau does) that *in a certain kind of society* promoting one's own interest is the same thing as promoting the public good,[9] and thus would have made room in his political system both for the duty to look well to one's own interests and that duty to promote the *public* interest which he demands of the members of his society. Or, to put the same point in another way, he would have seen that men must be related to one another in a certain way before we can conceive of their being willing to make this (first) of the three promises of which Locke is thinking[10]—and that, having posited the existence of such relations we must not, subsequently, exaggerate the extent to which their interests conflict.

With regard to the second and third of these understandings, the critic's most important task is to distinguish sharply between them; for, although they appear at first blush to come to much the same thing, they do not in fact do so. On the one hand Locke is saying (on our interpretation of the compact) that the idea of a society free from the inconvenience of the state of nature involves as a matter of course the recognition by the members of the society that the latter can act for the public good only by imposing certain uniformities of conduct upon its members, and that the members must stand ready to accept these impositions when they are in the public interest. There is, Locke is saying, an absolute and irrevocable obligation upon the members of a political

---

[7]Cf. Rousseau, *Contrat social,* i. 5: "Que des hommes épars soient successivement asservis à un seul . . . . je n'y vois point un peuple . . . . ; c'est, si l'on veut, une agrégation, mais non pas une association; *il n'y a là ni bien public, ni corps politique*" (italics mine). This is, clearly, to say that there are situations in which there is no good which is public.

[8]Cf. *ibid.,* ii. 1: "Si l'opposition des intérêts particuliers a rendu nécessaire l'établissement des sociétés, c'est l'accord de ces mêmes intérêts qui l'a rendu possible. C'est ce qu'il y a de commun dans ces différents intérêts qui forme le lien social; et s'il n'y avait pas quelque point dans lequel tous les intérêts s'accordent, nulle société ne saurait exister."

[9]*Ibid.,* ii. 4.

[10]Cf. viii. 107: "*Those who liked one another so well* as to join into society cannot but be supposed to have *some acquaintance and friendship* together, and some trust in one another" (italics mine).

society to discharge any duties which arise out of the community's needs, and to content themselves with such rights as attach to the performance of those duties. Implicit in this insistence is the notion that where men live together in a genuine community (*i.e.*, one with a good which is genuinely public) there arises a complex of rights which ought to be respected and duties which ought to be performed, and that the law of the community ought to be a law which enjoins those duties and respects those rights—which is, be it noted, some such restatement of the second thesis above as we have already warned the reader to expect. On the other hand, Locke is saying that a society free of the inconveniences of the state of nature is possible only where men can count upon each other to obey all positive legal enactments made in a certain way; and our point, for the moment, is that the promise necessary for an understanding of this kind is a promise of an essentially different character from the promise to promote the public good and the promise to obey that law which is in fact necessary for the promotion of that good. For, the moment we begin to speak of legal enactments made in a certain way, we move from the world of concepts into the world of actualities, where methods for enacting positive rules must, if they are to be applied, be applied by human beings who are not only fallible intellectually, thus capable of conceiving incorrectly the uniformities of conduct demanded by the public interest, but also capable, upon occasion, of employing for their own selfish purposes whatever power is entrusted to them to determine the content of legal enactments.

It is only against the background of the essential difference between the *first two* of these three understandings and the third (to which we shall devote most of the remainder of this chapter) that we can appreciate the significance of the question Locke raises, at the very beginning of his book, as to who the *persons* are who have the right of making laws, *i.e.*, who the persons are who have the right to political power. For such a question, on the lips of a man who believes that the *real* duty of each man in a political society is to promote the public good and to obey laws calculated to promote the public good is, quite simply, a *question mal posée*. The remainder of the present chapter is, in the main, an elaboration of this criticism of Locke. We do not propose to find fault with his assumption that the relations between the members of a political society free from the disadvantages of the state of nature can properly be described in contractual terms, or to raise inconvenient questions as to whether or not such a contract was ever negotiated by the members of any political society. We do not propose, either, to question his assumption that political society is necessary, in the sense explained above, or his assumption that by imposing upon its members duties disproportionate to benefits conferred, a society might well cease to be (or fail to become) a society free of the inconveniences of an unorganized existence, or his assumption that the *minima* of a society free of those inconveniences are a uniform law (thus one which imposes equal duties on its members), an impartial judge, and adequate machinery for the enforcement of its decrees. Nor shall we press further our objections, already recorded, to Locke's loose thinking about the public good, or his cavalier assumption that in promoting the good of one's own political platoon one also promotes the good of humankind. Rather we shall fix attention upon the relation between the *third* understanding, the notion that the members of a political society have promised one another absolute obedience to all positive enactments made in a certain way, and criticize it exclusively on Locke's own principles. It will be shown (1) that, although he did not use these words, Locke does read into this third understanding, not only the concept of unlimited sovereignty, but also the concept of an unlimited sovereignty which is *personal*; (2) that the promise necessary for such an understanding is prohibited by Locke's own theory of consent, thus would not (on his showing) be binding upon the members of his political society; and (3) that a society built upon such an understanding would not be free from the inconveniences which he attributes to the state of nature.

Most of the current misunderstandings about Locke's views on sovereignty can be attributed to (a) failure to distinguish between the powers of Locke's government (at any given moment) and the powers which (on his principles) the society can entrust to the government whenever it sees fit to do so, (b) failure to pay adequate attention to Locke's concrete proposals regarding political organization, (c) failure to face the implications of what Locke has to say about the right of revolution, and (d) failure to appreciate the character of the obligation which Locke assigns to the individual *vis-à-vis* his society and its law. We propose to take up these points *seriatim*.

(a) "The most significant thing about Locke's *Treatise of Civil Government*," writes Professor Lamprecht, "is really not what it says but what it avoids saying. Locke's most notable trait is that he could compose an entire treatise on government without so much as mentioning the word or introducing the idea of sovereignty."[11] And Professor Laski, whose opinion regarding a question of this kind cannot lightly be set aside, can be cited to the same effect. "It is," he says, "not accident which makes

[11]Lamprecht, "Hobbes and Hobbism," p. 49. Cf. *Id.*, *Moral and Political Philosophy of John Locke*, p. 148: "He did, to be sure, reject any government which does not rest on the consent of the governed; but he nowhere expounded a doctrine of popular sovereignty." Cf. Smith, *op. cit.*, p. 14: "The conception of the state which prevailed in the [American] Revolutionary period was very largely that which we find in the political writings of John Locke. His defense of the social compact was not a defense of unlimited power. . . . Sovereignty in the sense of unlimited power could have no place in the philosophy of the free state."

him [Locke] construct a non-sovereign state."[12] "His state is nothing so much as a contract between a group of business men who form a limited liability company whose memorandum of association forbids to the directors all those practices of which the Stuarts had, until his time, been guilty."[13] Furthermore, we have Locke's own word that "their [the legislative's] power in the utmost bounds of it is limited to the public good of the society. It is a power that hath no other end but preservation, and therefore can never have a right to destroy, enslave, or designedly to impoverish the subjects."[14] Now *one* clear meaning of these passages is that Locke intended the government *of the day* in his political society to be a government of limited power, thus of limited sovereignty, thus non-sovereign; and if this were all that Professors Lamprecht and Laski intended to say, the statements we have quoted from them above would be quite unexceptionable from the point of view of the present study. The relation between the government of the day in Locke's system and the society from which it derives its powers is, quite simply, assimilable to that between principal and agent in Anglo-American law; and for the government to claim *vis-à-vis* the society for which it acts powers which the society has not entrusted to it *would,* on Locke's showing, be as preposterous as for an agent to claim, *vis-à-vis* his principal, a freedom to do in the latter's name things which the latter does not wish done.[15]

Locke might, to be sure, have spoken more clearly about the precise character of the limits upon the power of the legislative (= the government)[16] and of the act by which it becomes the society's agent. There are passages from which, for example, we might get the impression that the legislative possesses a general power to take whatever action is necessary for the public good—a power similar to that which has, on occasion, been claimed for the government of the United States under the preamble and the general welfare clause of the constitution. The legislative may, he holds in such passages, "direct how the force of the commonwealth shall be employed for preserving the community and the members of it"[17]—a grant of power with which the most ambitious legislature might well be satisfied, and one which recalls the notion of "universal" agency in Anglo-American law. There are other passages which convey the impression (especially to an American reader, trained to think in such terms) that the legislative receives certain specific powers which—while it may not exceed them—it may subsequently exercise as a matter of right until

[12]Harold J. Laski, *The Rise of Liberalism* (New York: Harper & Brothers, 1936), p. 127.
[13]*Ibid.*
[14]xi. 135.
[15]Cf. Aaron, *op. cit.,* p. 273.
[16]Cf. xiii. 149: "In a constituted commonwealth . . . . acting for the preservation of the community, there can be but one supreme power, which is the legislative, to which all the rest are and must be subordinate."
[17]xii. 143.

it can be shown to have betrayed its trust. There are, again, passages in which critics have been able to see elements of a second, "governmental" *contract,* by which the society is itself bound not to disturb the legislature so long as it respects (the letter of? the spirit of?) the instrument of delegation.[18] "This legislative," he writes, "is not only the supreme power of the commonwealth, but sacred and unalterable in the hands where the community have once placed it."[19] And, again, the "legislative or supreme authority . . . . is *bound* to dispense justice and decide the rights of the subject by promulgated standing laws, and known authorised judges."[20] We return below to both these questions, but we may anticipate by saying that the notion of a right in the legislative to continue to govern so long as it can point to the language of such a contract as justification for its actions will hardly survive a careful reading of the *Second Treatise,*[21] and that Blackstone was undoubtedly correct (however misguided from the democratic point of view) when he denounced Locke for not having given to his government adequate protection against popular whims.[22]

It seems highly probable, however, that in these quotations Lamprecht and Laski meant to do more than deny the sovereignty of the government of the day in Locke's system, and that their intention was to identify Locke with that tendency in political theory which—carried out to its logical implications—eventuates in a demand for institutional limitations upon *all* governments, even governments acting under express popular mandate. If so, it can easily be shown that they have misunderstood the bearing of what Locke said about these matters, and have mistaken Locke's wish to limit the power of the agent (in the relation he is discussing) to act against the will of the principal for a wish to limit the power of the principal to give instructions to his agent. *I.e.,* the interesting question (which Lamprecht and Laski have answered incorrectly if they meant to answer it at all) is not whether the government in Locke's system has the power to do to the society that which the latter *disapproves,* but whether the society can assign to it the power to do that which the society *approves*—however much it may conflict with previously received notions regarding the limits upon government. Had they asked

---

[18]But cf. Gierke, *op. cit.,* pp. 104-105: "The doctrine of the social contract developed in England, especially in the sense of popular sovereignty. The English theory gave the contract of rulership only secondary importance *if it did not drop it altogether"* (italics mine). Cf. Wilson, *op. cit.,* p. 121.
[19]xi. 134.
[20]xi. 136 (italics mine).
[21]Cf. D. L. Keir, *The Constitutional History of Modern Britain, 1485-1937* (New York: D. Van Nostrand Co., 1938), p. 271. But cf. Lamprecht, *op. cit.,* p. 145: "The people [in Locke's system] as much as the legislative are morally bound to abide by the contract, and cannot, with changing whims, annul one contract to make another."
[22]Sir William Blackstone, *Commentaries on the Laws of England* (Philadelphia: J. B. Lippincott & Co., 1859), i. 213: "The principles of Mr. Locke . . . . would have reduced the society almost to a state of nature; would have levelled all distinctions of honour, rank, offices, and property; would have annihilated the sovereign power, and in consequence repealed all positive laws; and would have left the people at liberty to have erected a new system of state upon a new foundation of polity." This is strong evidence in favor of the interpretation of Locke urged in the present treatise.

themselves the second of these questions rather than the first, they would, as we shall show in (c) and (d) below, have used more cautious language in expounding Locke's ideas on sovereignty.[23]

(b) Nothing is easier, in writing about the *Second Treatise*,[24] than to forget that it is a book about politics and political institutions, and to proceed to treat it as if it were merely a book on ethics. All six of the aforementioned theses regarding the law of nature are, as we have shown, enunciated at some point in its argument; and none of them seems easy to square, at the limit, with the doctrine of unlimited sovereignty. We must, however, guard equally against the mistake of taking *one* of them as the doctrine of the "real" Locke and writing the others off as inconsistencies (for who can say which we should take?), and the mistake of confusing what we think he should (on his own ethical principles) have said about politics with what he in fact said. It is not improbable that behind the practical recommendations of every political theorist there lies a more or less articulate and more or less consistent theory as to what, in an ideal world, the limits upon governmental power ought to be. That governments should not violate the moral law, that they should not destroy or enslave or impoverish, that they should be stripped of authority when they begin to abuse it—these are propositions to which all (save only the perverse and sinful) who think about politics would unhesitatingly agree; and it is certain that Locke believed all of them. The differences between political theorists (in the light of which we distribute them into "schools") emerge when we consult them upon the *concrete institutional arrangements* which they are prepared to urge upon constitution-makers in a world in which the moral law must take its chances with the apparent necessity of placing the *legal* "right of making laws, with penalties of death and consequently all less penalties," in the hands of some person or group of persons—a world, furthermore, in which it is often difficult to decide whether or not a given law *is* one which destroys, enslaves, or impoverishes. Rules of morality and declarations of rights do get themselves written into constitutions, and perhaps, as Professor Laski maintains, it is well that they should.[25] But American experience with (*e.g.*) the so-called "penal clause" of the Fourteenth Amendment suggests that they affect the course of subsequent events only where (a) persons yet living demand that they be respected, and (b) power to enforce them happens to be in the hands of those persons and not others.[26] And in that background, the way to discover how

---

[23]Cf. Carpenter, *op. cit.*, p. 103: "In Locke's theory, sovereignty can exist nowhere except in the community as a whole. This is the original and supreme will which organizes the government and defines its just powers." Cf. John Neville Figgis, *The Divine Right of Kings* (Cambridge: University Press, 1914), p. 242.
[24]As the reader may see from Chapter IV above.
[25]Laski, *Grammar of Politics*, p. 305.
[26]Cf. *ibid.*, p. 103: "Rights are not merely, or even greatly, a matter of the written record. Musty parchments will doubtless give them greater sanctity; they will not ensure their realisation."

far a given political theorist is willing to go with the exponents of popular sovereignty is by fixing attention upon the facilities he would like to provide for the translation of popular will into governmental policy, and the facilities he would like to provide for preventing such translation when it might result in (*e.g.*) violation of the moral law, or action against the public good, *etc.* Locke never says, as Rousseau does,[27] that if a people wishes to do itself hurt no one has a right to prevent it from doing so, but his political system is that of a man who believes this; and as we shall see in (c) and (d) below, those seeking ammunition with which to defend America's peculiar institution will look in vain for it in the *Second Treatise.*[28]

(c) The drift of Locke's mind, where it concerns itself not with problems of pure right but those of right within the context of political organization, comes most clearly to light in those sections of the *Second Treatise* which deal with the right of revolution. It is in these sections that the significance of the limitations which he imposed upon his government may be seen in its most naked form. His doctrine is the simple one that "the community perpetually retains a supreme power of saving themselves from the attempts and designs of anybody, *even of their legislators,* wherever they shall be so foolish or so wicked as to lay and carry on designs against the liberties and properties of the subject";[29] that, in a word, "there remains . . . . in the people a supreme power to remove or alter the legislative, *when they find* the legislative act contrary to the trust reposed in them."[30]

The problem posed by such passages is, as we have pointed out above, that of the meaning we should assign to the word "trust." Lord, for example, finds in Locke only a "modified" right of revolution,[31] and Sabine sees in him what Rousseau was (he thinks) entitled to regard as an "unwarranted limitation on the power of the people to govern itself as it saw fit"—on the grounds, apparently, that the people, in Locke's system, can resume its power only by dissolving the government![32] It cannot, however, be too strongly emphasized that Locke, though sufficiently familiar with the idea of contract to base upon it his entire account of political obligation, uses another vocabulary in describing the relation between people and legislative, and that *he makes no*

---

[27]Rousseau, *op. cit.,* ii. 12.
[28]Cf. Louis B. Boudin, *Government by Judiciary* (New York: William Godwin, Inc., 1932), I, p. 82: "Clearly, Locke's opinions were not favorable to the establishment of government by judiciary; and . . . . the most influential of the Framers of the United States Constitution thought exactly as did Locke, both in the matter of the submission of the minority to the majority, as well as in the matter of there being 'no judge on earth' between the people and the Legislature, and the 'appeal to Heaven.' And, what is more to the point, they thought they had actually put Locke's doctrine into the Constitution."
[29]xiii. 149 (italics mine).
[30]*Ibid.* (italics mine).
[31]A. R. Lord, *The Principles of Politics* (Oxford: The Clarendon Press, 1921), p. 59.
[32]Sabine, *op. cit.,* p. 535. He sees in Locke the "persistence" of a tradition in which "a kind of indefeasibility in the right of the king and other governing organs" was regarded as compatible with "the right of a community to govern itself."

*secret of the fact that such reciprocal obligations as may be conceived to
have taken place between people and government are, at any given moment, merely what the people concede them to be.* In short, to think of
the "trust" by which the government acts as a contract is to think of a
contract whose terms are (by its own provision) to be interpreted unilaterally by one of the parties—*i.e.,* to deprive the term "contract" of
all of its ordinary meaning; and the critics have, in point of fact, been
overlooking the joker in Locke's description of the relation. To say that
the people can remove the legislative when they are of the opinion
(= "when they find")[33] that the legislative has acted against the public
good (= action "contrary to the trust reposed in them") is merely to say
that the character of that trust is defined from moment to moment by
what *we* are accustomed to call public opinion. Locke even goes so far as
to concede, at one point, that the solution which he is proposing for the
problems of politics involves laying "the foundation of government in the
. . . . opinion and . . . . humour of the people"![34]

Nor is this all that the critics have overlooked in Locke's account of
this matter. One of the passages reproduced above continues as follows:
"The trust must necessarily be forfeited, and the power devolve into the
hands of those that gave it, *who may place it anew where they shall think
best for their safety and security.*"[35] The right of revolution, that is to
say, involves a right to put in the place of the legislative against which it
is exercised one which *is* agreeable to the "opinion" and "humour" of the
people—a right in the people to formulate their own notions as to what is
"best for their safety and security" and, subsequently, to place power in
the hands of men who will use it in accordance with those notions.[36]

It is a matter of some interest that Dunning, whose interpretation of
Locke's theory coincides to a considerable extent with our own, finally
falls back into the very error from which he appears to have written
himself free. He says:

The society thus becomes, by the act of the individuals who form it, vested with
the function of determining what are offences against the law of nature, and
punishing violations of that law [wherefore anything is a violation of the law of
nature which the society chooses to define as such?].[37]

And, again:

As that which underlies government and becomes active only when government is
dissolved, the "community" [= the people?], ... is held always to be the

---

[33]Cf. xix. 240: "The people shall be judges." He is replying to his own question as to who
shall determine when a violation of the trust has occurred.
[34]xix. 223: "To this, perhaps, it will be said that the people being ignorant and always
discontented, to lay the foundation of government in the unsteady opinion and uncertain
humour of the people, is to expose it to certain ruin . . . . I answer . . . . [that] people are
not so easily got out of their old forms as some are apt to suggest."
[35]xiii. 149 (italics mine).
[36]Cf. xi. 141: "When the people have said, 'We will submit, and be governed by laws *made*
by such men* and in such forms,' nobody else can say other men shall make laws for them"
(italics mine).
[37]William Archibald Dunning, *A History of Political Theories from Luther to Montesquieu*
(New York: The Macmillan Co., 1905), pp. 349-350.

supreme power; . . . . supremacy . . . . belongs to that which is in the fullest sense the embodiment of [the public will of the society].[38]

So far in full agreement with our own interpretation; but not so in the sequel:

There is in this conception nothing of that absolute, unlimited, and uncontrollable sovereignty which was the soul of Hobbes' system.[39]

How are we to explain the fact that Dunning, having read Locke too carefully to attach to the limitations upon Locke's *government* the importance which they have assumed for other scholars, is yet unwilling to concede that what Locke ascribes to the society for which the government acts is *sovereignty?* Fortunately, Dunning has himself provided the answer to this question:

The natural rights of the individual limit the just power of the sovereign community precisely as they limited in the state of nature the just power of other individuals.[40]

In short, the explanation must be made in terms of the "persistence" of the notion (which we have already criticized in an earlier section) that Locke was, first, last, and always, the philosopher of inalienable individual rights. In the following section we shall examine the position of each of the individual members of Locke's political society *vis-à-vis* that society, attempting to show that the rights which he assigns to them are a function of, not a limitation on, the society's sovereignty.

(d) Before attempting to consider what Locke had to say about the obedience which the individual owes to the organized society of which he is a member, we must call attention to certain difficulties which the writer has deliberately ignored up to the present moment:

(1) We have, in the preceding section, taken no account of the possibility of differences of opinion between the members of a political society as to (*e.g.*) how it should employ its sovereignty, *i.e.*, its power of defining, and assessing penalties for, violations of the law of nature. We have, that is to say, simplified our discussion by equating the two questions: (a) what is the extent of the power which Locke claims for his political society? and (b) what is the extent of the power which Locke claims for the total membership of his political society—*i.e.*, for the people conceived in abstraction from the possibility of differences of opinion between them? Such a simplification has, be it noted, much to recommend it; since if we are to deal separately with the issues raised by the defenders of popular sovereignty (pure and simple) and those raised by the defenders of popular sovereignty plus majority-decisions regarding its exercise (= majority-sovereignty?) we must think, first of all, of a situation in

[38]*Ibid.*, p. 353.
[39]*Ibid.*, pp. 349-350. Cf. *ibid.*, p. 353: *So far as sovereignty is predicated by Locke* in fact, if not in name, it is ascribed to the collective body which is created by the social pact" (italics mine).
[40]*Ibid.*, p. 350.

which one might defend popular sovereignty without expressly committing oneself to majority-sovereignty; and the obvious example is a situation in which there *is* no dissident minority, thus unanimity. Or, to put the same thing in another way, we may tell ourselves that we have raised the question of the extent of the society's powers in its purest form when we state it with reference to a situation in which all methods of making decisions (except, possibly, decisions by lot)[41] about the use of those powers would come to the same thing. Purely aside, however, from the psychological improbability of unanimity, such a statement of the problem is unrealistic because all the interesting questions about the extent of a society's powers concern situations in which no problem would arise but for the *existence* of differences of opinion among its members. These questions are always, that is to say, questions as to what should be done when one of the society's members, or a group of its members, steps forward to insist that what is about to be done in the society's name *should* not be done (because unjust, unwise, unnecessary, or unprecedented)—a statement which, be it noted, applies equally to decisions about internal and external policy, since a society whose members are unanimous in their support of a given external policy can evidently adopt no other. Historically, therefore, attacks upon the doctrine of sovereignty have come always from those who would like to make it possible for individuals and groups of individuals to prevent the action contemplated at such moments; and we are brought face to face with the curiosity that while we can (and must) distinguish between popular sovereignty and majority-sovereignty, by conceiving of the former in terms of unanimity, any particular exercise of popular sovereignty either ranges some of the society's members against others, thus (save in the improbable case of an unbreakable tie) a majority of those members against a minority, or poses no problem for theory to solve. Since, however, it is easy to conceive of arrangements whereby the power to make decisions regarding the exercise of the society's powers has been entrusted to a minority, the necessity of distinguishing between the sovereignty of the society and the sovereignty of the majority remains.

The simplification is further recommended by the fact that (along with the difficulty it involves) it is Locke's own—*i.e.*, he treats as a discrete question the claims of the majority of its members to exercise the power he attributes to the whole, and, in such a passage as that reproduced on page 99 above, he is clearly treating the society as (constructively) unanimous *although* the members of the legislative are evidently members of the society.[42]

---

[41]"Possibly," because it appears improbable that a decision which nobody favors will be enforced.

[42]Cf. Aaron, *op. cit.*, p. 276: "On . . . . [Locke's] view the contract is between all the members of the society, as a consequence of which a trust is imposed upon one or more individuals. The ruler does not stand opposite to the people; he is one of them, but entrusted with exceptional duties."

(2) Locke was not especially concerned, in connection with his theory of popular sovereignty, with the problem for which (as we have just pointed out) modern liberalism has sought a solution, namely, that of the limits of the society's power over the individual member *as such* (rather than as an official of the society)—any more than, in his discussion of the majority's power over the minority, he was concerned with the question of possible abuse by a governing majority of its power over a governed minority. As Professor Lerner has lately reminded us, we live in a period in which things have happened to *governed* minorities and individuals which oblige us to give careful consideration to the problem of how they may be protected against "tyrannical" majorities.[43] Locke, in contrast, had clearly been seized of that which in his day was happening to governed majorities at the hands of minorities and individuals, and it was in this form that the problem involved most readily presented itself to his mind. Nevertheless, as we are about to show, he puts forward propositions which commit him on the issue as we discuss it today, and it is to these propositions that we direct the reader's attention in the following paragraphs:

Locke's teaching on this point is, quite simply, that which (erroneously, in the present writer's opinion) is usually attributed to Rousseau: The individual owes to the commonwealth of which he is a member a duty of obedience which is absolute and perpetual, and *must* be absolute and perpetual because the alternative is the anarchy of the state of nature:

The power that every individual gave the society when he entered into it can never revert to the individuals again, as long as the society lasts, but will always remain in the community; because without this there can be no community—no commonwealth.[44]

The power which the individual "gave up" includes *both* his power to "do whatever he thinks fit for the preservation of himself and others"[45] and his "power of punishing"[46]—and he gives them up, according to Locke, with the understanding that they are both to be exercised by the society,[47] which can subsequently call upon him to assist in the enforcement of its laws:

He has given up a right to the commonwealth to employ his force for the execution of the judgments of the commonwealth whenever he shall be called to it,

---

[43]Although minorities have surely suffered least in the only country which has entrusted unlimited power to the numerical majority of its citizens. Cf. Lerner, *op. cit.*, p. 107: "What has happened to minorities in our day makes many of us fear majorities." Cf. Saripolos, *op. cit.*, p. 268: "Aujourd'hui, à la fin du XIXe siècle, il s'agit en fin de fonder la vraie liberté et de protéger la minorité contre les *privilèges* de la majorité. La minorité demande aujourd'hui, comme la majorité avant la Révolution, à être quelque chose."

[44]xix. 243. Cf. Rousseau, *op. cit.*, i. 6, where we are told that the contract remains in force only "jusqu'à ce que, le pacte social étant violé, chacun rentre alors dans ses premiers droits, et reprenne sa liberté naturelle."

[45]Not, as Dunning incorrectly supposes, one power only. The misunderstanding is apparently due to Locke's unfamiliar use of the word "single" in the sentence (ix. 127): "It is this makes them so willingly give up every one his *single* [= private?] power of punishing, *etc.*" Cf. Dunning, *op. cit.*, p. 349.

[46]ix. 128.

[47]ix. 130.

which, indeed, are his own judgments, they being made by himself or his representative.[48]

Furthermore,

. . . . every man when he at first incorporates himself into any commonwealth, he, by his uniting himself thereunto, annexes also, and submits to the community *those possessions which he has, or shall acquire,* that do not already belong to any other government. . . . They become, both . . . . person and possession, subject to the government and dominion of that commonwealth as long as it hath a being.[49]

Translated into the political vocabulary of our own day, these statements say as unambiguously as possible that (whatever may be the position of the individual *vis-à-vis* a *government* which he believes to have violated its trust and thus to have surrendered its title to act in the name of the commonwealth)[50] where the government's title to act in the name of the commonwealth is beyond dispute (or where the community itself acts as a legislature), the individual's rights (including his rights of property) are merely those vouchsafed to him by the positive law of his society. The individual may feel that a given law infringes upon his "natural" rights (*i.e.,* that it is morally outrageous), or that it is directed to some other end than "the peace, safety, and public good of the people";[51] but he cannot withhold his obedience, because membership in a commonwealth involves as a matter of course the surrender both of his private judgment and of his power to act upon his convictions. If, for example, he is a Quaker, and the law with which he is confronted is a declaration of war which provides for conscription, it becomes his duty not only to participate in the hostilities, but also, if called upon to do so, to assist in the coercion of conscientious objectors. Thus, while Carritt can find ample support in the *Second Treatise* for his statement to the effect that Locke "is one of those who think we ought to obey a government so long as it on the whole secures justice and happiness,"[52] he should not have gone on to say, on the strength of that statement, that "with all . . . . [its] faults . . . . his account of political obligation seems to me the best."[53] For in saying this he not only overlooks the major implications of Locke's real theory of *political* obligation (= that which describes the individual's obligation to the political unit of which he is a member), but also absolves Locke from responsibility for the introduction into modern political theory of the dangerous equivocation which was finally to develop into what Hobhouse has called the "meta-

---

[48]vii. 88 (italics mine). Cf. vii. 89: "He authorises the society, or which is all one, the legislative thereof, to make laws for him as the public good of the society shall require, to the execution whereof his own assistance (as to his own decrees) is due." Cf. ix. 130.
[49]viii. 120 (italics mine).
[50]The reservation is necessary because Locke clearly intended that the commonwealth should regard itself as free to alter its government by revolution, and the revolution would of necessity be made by individuals.
[51]ix. 131.
[52]Carritt, *Morals and Politics,* p. 79.
[53]*Ibid.*

physical theory of the state."[54] For Locke (as we have seen) is saying, before Rousseau, two centuries before Bosanquet, that the commonwealth's judgments (= its laws = its will[55]) are the individual's own judgments (= his will), and is saying it in such fashion as to suggest that they are the individual's judgments *whether he agrees with them or not, i.e., they are the individual's judgments even when he consciously disagrees with them.* Nor can it be argued that this is to read into a single passage a meaning which is at variance with the remainder of Locke's argument, for he must be very deaf indeed to the nuances of political discourse who cannot detect in the following lines the elements of the distinction between the "actual" will of the individual and the "real" will which is his whether he thinks it is or not, as also of the insistence that freedom consists rather in the presence than the absence of constraint (*i.e.,* the insistence which Hobhouse treats as the essence of the "metaphysical" theory):

Law, in its true notion, is not so much the limitation as the direction of a free and intelligent agent to his proper interest [even when it directs him to that which he regards as against his interest?]. . . . That ill deserves the name of confinement which hedges us in only from bogs and precipices. . . . The end of law is not to abolish or restrain, but to preserve and enlarge freedom.[56]

Locke's use of the word "law" is, to be sure, ambiguous in the extreme, since it means now the positive law and now that which the positive law ought to be (= the law of nature) ; but since in the discussion cited he says "this holds in all the laws a man is under, whether natural or civil,"[57] we are entitled to suppose that it provides a reliable index to Locke's opinions regarding the individual's right to call into question the binding character of the law of his community.[58]

It is interesting to notice, in this background, that Locke, like more recent writers whose minds have run to an absolute obligation on the part of the individual to regard the will of his community as his own will, does not hesitate to press *à l'outrance* the analogy between the relation of the community to its members and the relation of the organism to its parts. "When," he writes, "any number of men have so consented to make one community or government, they are thereby presently incorporated, and make one body politic" ;[59] and political power is "that power

---

[54]L. T. Hobhouse, *The Metaphysical Theory of the State* (London: G. Allen & Unwin, 1918).
[55]xiii. 151.
[56]vi. 57.
[57]vi. 59.
[58]Cf. *ibid.*: "Is a man under the law of England? what made him free of that law— that is, to have the liberty to dispose of his actions and possessions, according to his own will, within the permission of that law? *a capacity of knowing that law"* (italics mine). Thus he can argue, a few lines later, (vi. 60) that whilst he is incapable of "knowing the law, and so living within the rules of it," a man should be "continued under the tuition and government of others." This is, evidently, to say that the individual may take his choice between being treated like a child, on the one hand, and making his will conform to the law of the community, on the other hand.
[59]95. Cf. Rousseau, *op. cit.,* iv. 1: "Tant que plusieurs hommes réunis se considèrent comme un seul corps, ils n'ont qu'une seule volonté." *I.e.,* so long as a group of men have a single will they have a single will—a statement which is less startling than Locke's, but somewhat more convincing.

. . . . to make laws and annex such penalties to them as may tend to the preservation of the whole, by cutting off those parts, and those only, which are so corrupt that they threaten the sound and healthy, without which no severity is lawful."[60] Such a passage, furthermore, gives us the most concise answer we shall find to the question raised in the present chapter: Even the individual's right to life is valid only to the extent that it is compatible with the good (= preservation) of his community, and it is the people, not the individual, to whom Locke has clearly imputed the power to make the necessary judgments as to what is compatible with its preservation.[61] This, then, is our reply to Dunning: If that which Locke claims for his community is not unlimited sovereignty, where would one turn, in the literature of politics, to find a sovereignty which *is* unlimited?[62]

We now have before us the main elements of the individual promise which is presupposed by Locke's theory of popular sovereignty; and we may, without injustice to his argument, proceed at once to the line of criticism which we propose to direct against it. The individual has, it must be remembered, made the promise in order to escape the inconveniences which attach to existence outside an organized society: uncertainty as to the nature of his own rights and duties, and those of other men, inadequate guarantees of impartial arbitration where differences of opinion arise between him and other men, insufficient machinery for the enforcement of his rights when the law is on his side. So long, therefore, as the individual is able to see that he has got a good bargain, that by keeping the promise he is in fact looking, in the best possible manner, to his own preservation and welfare, and insofar as Locke is prepared to overlook the second thesis above and stand by the first, the most that can be said about the promise he describes is that it is unnecessary— since under the first thesis he is apparently obligated to keep good bargains whether he has promised to or not. But, as we have now seen at some length, the promise is to be kept even when the bargain turns out badly, and involves a previous commitment by the individual to accept the verdict of the remaining members of the society with regard to every difference of opinion between himself and them on matters of right; and (leaving to one side the first thesis and concentrating now on the fifth) he has made himself accountable for a demonstration that, in the presence

---

[60] xv. 171. Cf. Rousseau, *De l'économie politique*, pp. 25-26, where he condemns this notion as "une des plus exécrables que jamais la tyrannie ait inventées."

[61] Cf. Aaron, *op. cit.*, p. 287: "Locke is an individualist, and yet his individualism is left undefined; for no definite solution is to be found in his works of the vexed problem of the relations between the individual and the community."

[62] Bearing in mind the fact that Lamprecht is one of the critics who have found in Locke no trace of the idea of sovereignty, the reader may profitably compare the account we have just given of the power of Locke's community over the individual with what, in another writer, Lamprecht regards as "absolutism" (*op. cit.*, p. 45): "While even Hobbes exempted men from obeying commands which ordered them to take their own lives or to give up their means of livelihood, Filmer refused to tolerate such slight exemptions. In Filmer the absolutism of the monarch reaches its most extreme statement."

of such a difference, the remaining members of the society will exercise their power *impartially*. That is, Locke must either show us that the remaining members of the society will, at such a moment, judge impartially, in which case the promise to obey was one which the individual could rightfully make and ought therefore to keep, or he must admit that his theory represents each individual as having subjected himself to the absolute, arbitrary will of the remaining members. In the latter case the promise would not (on Locke's showing) be a binding one.

What we cannot permit Locke to do, in all this, is to surround his doctrine regarding the society's sovereignty over the individual with the atmosphere of reasonableness and impersonality which attaches, superficially at least, to arrangements calling for decisions in accordance with the unanimity-principle—a principle to which Locke makes his appeal every time he says that a man can be bound only by his own consent. Or (what comes to the same thing) we must now demand of him that he pay the price for his attempt to have it more ways than one with his law of nature. According to the first thesis, the individual's obligation (thus also the society's sovereignty) would necessarily cease at that moment when further discharge of the obligation would clearly militate against preservation of his life, liberty, and estate. According to the sixth thesis, a man cannot give up his power to resist force when, in his own opinion, it is exerted upon him without right; and Locke clearly wants to reply that the question does not arise with regard to coercion by the community, because the right flows from the individual's own previous consent. When, however, we take him at his word about this, and proceed to examine what he has to say about consent, we discover (a) that the individual is represented as having consented only to the exercise of impartial authority, and thus, apparently, would not be bound to obey community authority when exercised in a partial manner, and (b) that the individual has, in Locke's belief, no right to consent to authority of any other kind. The obvious solution to the difficulty would evidently have been to propose a political system in which, as in his state of nature, laws would be made and governmental arrangements established only with unanimous approval, and subsequently changed only by unanimous approval—*i.e.*, approximately the kind of system which Burke defends. When, under such a system, the individual finds himself the victim of what be believes to be an unjust law, he can at least be reminded that he has himself, in a cool moment, set his seal to its reasonableness, and that, in any case, nothing can be changed in a sense unfavorable to himself except with his own approval. Locke was logically estopped from proposing such a system by the insight which we have presented as his fourth thesis—*i.e.*, by the knowledge that today's justice may be to-

morrow's injustice because of a change of conditions; and, evidently with
a view to preventing the indefinite perpetuation of ancient enactments
which are no longer defensible, he proceeds to shift his ground from
unanimity at some moment in the past as an ultimate criterion of right
to virtual unanimity (either in the present or at some time in the past) as
an ultimate criterion of right. The society can come into existence only
by unanimous approval of its members; but subsequently, by making a
revolution, the people (no longer represented as strictly unanimous) may
change the society's character in any way they see fit, and require of the
individual (*e.g.*, the individual member of the legislative they have
turned out) the same duty of obedience which he owed before the
revolution. The people have, in short, consented unanimously to something less than unanimity as an ultimate criterion of right; and Locke
is evidently asserting that such consent is valid.[63]

The issue posed here may be stated very simply indeed, and since it
is, in effect, the Great Divide which separates the defenders of popular
sovereignty from their opponents (and, ultimately, the defenders of
majority-rule from their opponents), we shall be well advised to grasp it
as clearly as possible at this point. Here are a group of people united
together in order to enjoy the benefits of just and reasonable government. A difference arises amongst them as to what is just and reasonable, and investigation reveals that the opposing factions consist of one
individual, on the one side, and the remainder of the community, on the
other side. Does either have a *right* to impose its view of what is just and
reasonable upon the other? Can either judge impartially in what is, by
definition, its own cause? Locke's theory of popular sovereignty obliges
him to answer the second question in the affirmative, and the first with
the words, Yes, the rest of the community has such a right.[64] And, since
the only difference between the two (the community minus one of its
members, and the individual) which leaps to the eye is that the one
is many individuals and the latter is only one, he is obliged to say that
numbers guarantee impartiality.

An ocean separates those who, confronted with the above problem,
are willing to make Locke's answer, and those whose cast of mind makes
it necessary for them to argue that no answer can be given on the facts

[63]Here, again, Rousseau is much the more cautious of the two. Cf. Rousseau, *Contrat social*, i. 6: "La loi de la pluralité des suffrages est . . . . un établissement de convention, et suppose, *au moins* une fois, l'unanimité" (italics mine).
[64]Cf. *ibid.*, ii. 4: "En effet, sitôt qu'il s'agit d'un fait ou d'un droit particulier sur un point qui n'a pas été réglé par une convention générale et antérieure, l'affaire devient con-tentieuse. C'est un procès où les particuliers intéressés sont une des parties, et le public l'autre, mais où *je ne vois ni la loi qu'il faut suivre, ni le juge qui doit prononcer*" (italics mine). It is interesting to notice that Professor Friedrich, who, as we have seen, regards Rousseau as in some sense responsible for the excesses of those who attach too much importance to "approximate majority support," is in this matter (as Rousseau clearly was not) a thorough-going majoritarian. Cf. Friedrich, *Constitutional Government and Politics*, p. 454: "The narrower the special interest is, the lower is the representative quality of those whose actions are directed towards its realiza-tion. And an interest is narrow or broad depending on the *number* of human beings whose interest is identified with it" (italics mine).

stated—*i.e.*, that the community may be right, or the individual may be right, or they both may be wrong. (We repeat that Locke cannot seriously contend that the community is right because the individual has promised to regard it so, because unless there be reasons for regarding the community as right [= impartial] at such a moment, the promise is not a valid one.) We make no attempt to adjudicate the issue at stake, our purpose being merely to show what position Locke finally adopted with regard to it and what consequences the position involves for the consistency of his argument. And the charge we are bringing against him is that he has attempted to argue from unanimity as a criterion of right (a criterion which is, in some sense, consistent with the fifth thesis) to constructive, or virtual, unanimity (as revealed in his discussion of the right of revolution) as an equally acceptable criterion of right. If Locke had stayed with the unanimity-principle, we are saying, he would have made no distinction between a situation in which an individual wishes to alter existing arrangements, and one in which all individuals except one wish to alter them; for under the rule *pacta sunt servanda* the two situations are indistinguishable, the individual having the same right of revolution against the society as the society has against the individual, which is none at all. And we are insisting that Locke's right of revolution is, in effect, a right on the part of the bulk of the community to treat as non-members those who take exception to its opinions, a right which is wholly inconsistent with the fifth thesis.

There is much to be said against the unanimity-principle as a criterion of right in an organized society, but there is this to be said in its favor: that where action can be taken under it at all there is some sort of presumption that the action taken is the wisest and most reasonable of which the deliberators are, as a group, capable. Every disputant among them must have been heard and convinced before action becomes possible; every suggestion that the action about to be taken is unwise or unjust must have been refuted to the satisfaction of him who has put it forward. By providing a maximum of guarantees against new decisions of all kinds, it provides a maximum of guarantees against new decisions which are unwise or unjust. Thus, although unanimous decisions do become unanimous only by the accumulation of individual approvals, they do not owe their peculiar quality to the *number* of the approvals—or, at least, the further claim may be made for them that they are underwritten by the reasoning process itself insofar as the deliberators in question are capable of reasoning. The unanimity-principle, that is to say, forces the deliberators to observe the basic rules of the reasoning process: consideration of all evidence available, attribution of equal weight to all points of view, *etc.*; and of decisions made under it we may say not only that they have secured general approval, but also (with *some* confidence)[65] that they have been able to withstand all the criticisms urged against them by all the minds consulted with respect to them—which is apparently the most that can be said for any decision at any particular moment. This is important because those who take inadequate notice of this characteristic of unanimous decisions yield easily to the temptation of arguing that since unanimous decisions are best, almost unanimous decisions are next best, and thus the best possible where complete unanimity cannot be secured. The only theorist whom the writer has found ready to put this argument forward thus unambiguously is Starosolskyj;[66] but the ease with which Locke makes the transition from the one position to the other in his theory of sovereignty suggests that he had something of this kind in mind, and it cannot be too strongly emphasized that *there is no connection between the premise and the conclusion.* Where there is virtual unanimity only there is opposition, *i.e.,* there are unsatisfied objectors, *i.e.,* minds which, by withholding approval, create a presumption against the decision—a presumption whose strength bears no demonstrable relation to the number of the unsatisfied objectors, and one which all of us have seen vindicated with disturbing frequency in situations in which the objectors have been few. The arguments in favor of the unanimity-principle cannot, therefore, be applied *a fortiori* to the defense of virtually unanimous decisions, because the distinctive quality of unanimous decisions is not a quality of which decisions may partake to a greater or lesser degree; either, that is to say, all the objections have been answered or they have not. This is not to say, of course, that the principle of unanimity is a better principle for political societies to adopt than a principle requiring only virtual unanimity, or that the right of nearly all the members of a commonwealth to revoke previous decisions is less susceptible of defense than that of all the members. What we can say is (a) that Locke could have claimed for decisions made under the *liberum veto* something of the impartiality and impersonality which would legitimate (under the fifth thesis) the promise which he demands of the members of his society, and (b) that the right of *nearly all* must be defended on different grounds than that of all. But Locke's attempts to find such grounds—as we shall encounter them in the next chapter—are remarkably unsuccessful, and as we present him here he is either not arguing at all (*i.e.,* merely asserting) or arguing (on what level of awareness we do not endeavor to say) from the proposition that all (thus also the few) are bound by that to which all *have* consented, to the proposition that the few are bound by that to which the rest *have consented* (as after a revolu-

---

[65]With *some* confidence only, because of the possibility that objections have been withdrawn by objectors who, though by no means satisfied, have yet despaired of convincing others and are unwilling to stand in the way of action.
[66]Starosolskyj, *op. cit.,* p. 56.

tion), and thence to the proposition that the few are bound by that to which the rest *now consent*—wherefore he can insist, as he does, that the government which calls down on itself a revolution is itself rebellious, the "law" presumably having changed at the moment when the society (= the members minus the government and its supporters) recognized the necessity for making one.[67] Neither of these steps is legitimate.

Locke's failure to take account of the above difficulty is astonishing, but less astonishing, on the whole, than his failure to offer the sort of defense for the (virtually unanimous) community's right of revolution that we should expect from him in the light of his usual handling of the subject of rights and duties. As we have seen in an earlier chapter, Locke elsewhere reveals a profound insight into the problem of rights and duties, representing the former as, in a manner of speaking, merely another way of looking at the latter, and both as determined by a common or collective good. If, therefore, he proposes to speak in terms of a duty in the individual to obey the rest of his community and a right in the rest of the community to coerce the individual, he should tell us not only why the individual has (as compared to the rest of the community) that lesser duty to promote the public good which is the correlative of his lesser right to make laws and use the force of the community in its behalf, but also why the concession to the bulk of the community of a right to remove and install governments should result in the promotion of the public good. The latter problem would have led him into an analysis of that public opinion which he briefly mentions, and of the relation between the public good and widely-received opinion as to what is good. But neither problem appears to have occurred to him, and we are obliged, therefore, to urge against the right he claims for the bulk of the community the objection that it will not bear examination in the light of his own theory of rights.

[67]xix. 226.

Chapter VII

THE RIGHT OF THE MAJORITY

> When any number of men have . . . . consented to make one
> community or government . . . . the majority have a right to
> act and conclude the rest.[1]

THIS IS Locke's clearest statement of his doctrine regarding what we
have called in our Introduction the majority-principle, and it is, be it
noted, so phrased as to fit very neatly into our interpretation of the compact. Wherever men live in community with one another, he is saying,
the relations between them can be described in terms of an agreement
which, in addition to assigning to the whole community that unlimited
power which we have examined in the preceding section, assigns to its
numerical majority a *right* to make decisions (regarding the use of that
power) which are binding upon the minority. The majority-principle is,
in a word, implicit in the logic of community life.

It is not only Locke's clearest commitment to the use of the majority-
principle, but also the most concise statement of the faith of the majority-
rule democrat that the present writer has been able to find in the course
of his investigation; and we shall greatly clarify the problem of the
present section if we face at once all that it implies. Assuming—as, in
the context in which it is claimed, we must assume—that the right to
which the statement refers is an ethical right, then it necessarily follows
that decisions made by the majority (= action taken by the majority)
are in some definable sense ethically right decisions, since, in the absence
of convicing proof to the contrary, it is necessary to suppose that there
can be no such thing as an ethical right to make an ethically wrong
decision. It follows, again, that any decision other than that of the
majority is in some definable sense ethically wrong. It follows, yet again,
that a decision comes to be right the moment it marshals majority support
behind it, and ceases to be right the moment the "marginal" deliberator
switches sides and reduces the erstwhile majority to a minority. And
since these corollaries do clearly follow from it, it is to Locke, not to any
recent writer, that Professor Friedrich should give credit for a "statement of the majoritarian position" which "avoids all subterfuges."[2]

We shall greatly clarify our problem, too, by facing at once the
implications of Locke's proposition about the right of the majority with
regard to the questions dealt with in the preceding sections. The indi-

---

[1]vii. 95.
[2]Friedrich, "One Majority Against Another," p. 43. Cf. Vaughan, *op. cit.*, I, p. 166:
"This [Locke's statement on the power of the majority] amounts to a blank cheque drawn in
favour of 'the majority,' and eventually filled up either to tens or millions, as fortune may
decide."

vidual has, as we have seen, an irrevocable obligation to obey the community of which he is a member; <u>but the majority has a right to act for the community</u>; and the individual's irrevocable duty of obedience thus turns out to be <u>an irrevocable duty to obey the majority.</u> The inalienable rights of the individual are, as we have seen, such rights as may be compatible with the public good of his society, and, as we have further seen, that public good is merely that which the "opinion" and "humour" of the people designate as good; but since the majority of those people have a right to conclude the rest, the inalienable rights of the individual prove to be merely those which the majority of the people have not yet seen fit to withdraw.[3] The "proper interest" of each individual lies in obedience to a law decreed by a legislative which, as we have seen, is presumed to enjoy the confidence of the community; but since the majority can act for the community, and can thus exercise the community's right of revolution and its right to replace the old government with a new one to its liking, the proper interest of the individual becomes merely unquestioning obedience to the will of the majority. Here, in short, is the Rousseauism which is nowhere to be found in the *Contrat social* and the *Gouvernement de Pologne*; and it is a matter of no little interest that Locke, apparently because the platitudes about morals which we have examined in the opening sections of this chapter cannot be squared with such a position, has got off with so little responsibility for the introduction of such notions into modern political theory.[4]

We now turn to consider the arguments by which Locke supports this proposition.[5]

First Argument. The right to live under a government agreeable to the majority is a natural right of all men—or, in Locke's own language, men have a "native right . . . . to have such a legislative over them as the majority should approve and freely acquiesce in."[6] This Locke does not seek to demonstrate; and we need only take notice of its presence in

[3]But cf. Wilson, *op. cit.*, pp. 218-219: "Locke's *Two Treatises* put above the rough determination of majority vote the immutable natural rights of man."

[4]Thus Vaughan, who in view of the comment reproduced in n. 2 above, can hardly be accused of having *overlooked* the majoritarian emphasis in Locke's theory, yet clings to the notion that that theory is "not merely anti-despotic, but also markedly individualist" (*op. cit.*, I, p. 134). "*The Essay of Civil Government*," he writes (*ibid.*), "is . . . an assault . . . . upon the very idea of sovereignty. Its shafts are aimed not merely against one particular form of sovereignty—doubtless the most oppressive and the least endurable—but against any form [thus against "blank cheques" to majorities?], even the mildest, that sovereignty can assume." Locke pleads for toleration for all save atheists and Catholics, and wins a reputation for having exercised "considerable" influence in "advancing the cause of toleration" (Lamprecht, *op. cit.*, p. 152); Rousseau pleads (*Contrat social*, iv. 8) for toleration for all save atheists and Catholics, and Vaughan (*The Political Writings of Rousseau* [Cambridge: University Press, 1915], I, p. 89) accuses him of advocating persecution. Rousseau writes (*op. cit.*, iv. 2) that provided "tous les caractères de la volonté générale sont encore dans la pluralité," I am more free when subjecting myself to the will of the majority than I would have been had I got my way—and wins recognition as a majoritarian! Locke, with no limiting conditions at all, equates the consent of the individual with that of the majority, and wins recognition as an individualist! Cf. Locke, xi. 140: "Governments cannot be supported without great charge, and it is fit everyone . . . . should pay out of his estate his proportion for the maintenance of it. *But still it must be with his own consent, i.e., the consent of the majority*" (italics mine).

[5]It is instructive to notice that there is absolutely nothing in the *Contrat social* which can properly be called an argument for majority-right.

[6]xvi. 176. The writer has not attempted to list Locke's arguments in the order in which he introduces them.

the *Second Treatise* and remind the reader of Ritchie's pleasantry[7] to the effect that the maxim, "No case; talk about the law of nature," plays in the profession of political theory a rôle analogous to that of the maxim, "No case; abuse plaintiff's attorney," in the practice of law.[8]

Second Argument. If the minority refused to be concluded by the majority, the society would speedily disintegrate; for, he insists, the only alternative is the unanimity-principle (= "nothing but the consent of every individual can make anything to be the act of the whole"[9]) ; and both because it is frequently impossible to consult everybody[10] and because "variety of opinions and contrariety of interests . . . . unavoidably happen in all collections of men,"[11] such a principle would deprive the society of the strength it needs in order to fulfill the purposes for which it was created.[12] In short, "where the majority cannot conclude the rest, there they cannot act as one body, and consequently will be immediately dissolved again."[13]

This we may call the argument from *necessity and expediency,*[14] and the importance it has assumed in subsequent discussion of the case for majority-decisions is the most interesting indication we possess of the need for investigation of the problem by competent theorists. It is open to the following obvious objections:

(a) It is simply not true that a commonwealth must choose between decisions by majority-vote and dissolution after a brief period of experiment with unanimous decisions, since, as Locke must have known very well, the power to make decisions binding upon all of its members may (and often does) become lodged in a minority of the society's members. That is, Locke's dilemma is, in the form in which he states it, a false dilemma.

(b) If it *were* true that the society must choose between dissolution and the lodgment of decision-making power in the majority, this would not constitute a valid argument in favor of the proposition that wherever men have "consented to make a community," the majority have a right to make that community's decisions. Even conceding the inarticulate premise that all commonwealths have a right to continue in existence and to thrive, the most that can be deduced from it is a decision-making right in that part of each commonwealth which is in fact most capable of assuring to it a healthy existence. It is possible to conceive of circum-

---

[7]David G. Ritchie, *Natural Rights* (London: Swan Sonnenschein and Co., 1895), p. 31.
[8]Cf. Vaughan, *Studies,* I, pp. 140-141: "The answer of Locke is perfectly explicit: Those who make a social contract bind themselves to . . . . regulate all their future proceedings by a bare majority: a provision imposed by that accommodating oracle, the law of nature, whose commands form the strangest assortment, ranging from *Thou shalt not kill* to *The odd man shall have the casting vote.*"
[9]viii. 98.
[10]Cf. *ibid.*: "Infirmities of health and avocations of business . . . . will necessarily keep many away from the public assembly."
[11]*Ibid.*
[12]*Ibid.*
[13]*Ibid.*
[14]Cf. Wilson, *op. cit.,* p. 64: "Locke in his *Second Treatise* defends majority rule primarily on the ground of expediency, for without it civil society could not endure."

stances in which such a right might, on this showing, vest in the majority, but it is also possible to conceive of circumstances in which the majority-principle would conduce directly to the commonwealth's ruin. In such a case (leaving to one side the ever-present possibility of minority-rule) dissolution and majority-rule would appear to be equally undesirable.

For the rest, it seems improbable that the premise, according to which all commonwealths to which men happen at some time to have given their "consent," have a right to continue in existence and to thrive, can be successfully defended.

For all of its absurdity, in the form in which Locke states it, the argument contains the elements of a proposition which—although it still awaits its theorist—deserves (in the present writer's opinion) serious consideration as the point of departure for theoretically sound treatment of the majority-principle. For if, instead of saying that the society must either entrust decision-making power to the majority or face speedy dissolution, he had said that it must either entrust the decision-making power to the majority or cease to be *a society in which all can participate in the making of decisions,* he would not only have enunciated a proposition which cannot be so easily refuted as that which he does put forward, but also would have set his successors in the modern debate about majority-rule a problem worthy of their best speculative efforts.

Third Argument. Denial of the right of the majority to conclude the minority would deprive the commonwealth of its title to govern.[15]

That which begins and actually constitutes any political society is nothing but the consent of any number of freemen capable of majority, to unite and incorporate into such a society [*i.e.,* one in which all necessary power has been given up to the majority] . . . . This is that, and that only, which did or could give beginning to any lawful government in the world.[16]

Here, again, Locke is apparently very close to the idea which we have set forth at the end of our discussion of the second argument, and seems about to say that there are demonstrable differences between a society which does and one which does not make its decisions by majority-vote[17]—and differences which, from the ethical point of view, render the

---

[15]It is interesting to note the use which the members of a minority (in a society governed in accordance with Locke's ideas about majority-rule) might make of one of his pronouncements on absolute monarchy—*e.g.,* vii. 90-91: "Absolute monarchy . . . . is indeed inconsistent with civil society, and so can be no form of civil government at all . . . . [The absolute prince] being supposed to have all . . . . power in himself alone, there is no judge to be found, no appeal lies open to any one, who may fairly and indifferently, and with authority decide, and from whence relief and redress may be expected of any injury or inconveniency that may be suffered from him, or by his order."

[16]viii. 99.

[17]It is on this level that Starosolskyj attacks the problem of majority-decisions. His book—the best we have on the subject—is an effort to demonstrate the theoretically necessary differences between what he calls the *Mehrheitsverband* and what he calls the *Herrschaftsverband* (*op. cit.,* pp. 22-34). Unfortunately, he defines the *Mehrheitsverband* in such fashion as to exclude any organization in which there exists a crystallized majority—*i.e.,* any organization in which the relations of subordination and superordination have ceased to be "indeterminate" (*ibid.,* p. 33). This means, of course, that the difference between the *Mehrheitsverband* and the *Herrschaftsverband* does not, at the limit, turn at all upon the fact that in the one decisions are made by the majority and in the other by an individual or a minority. Nevertheless, Starosolskyj has pointed the way to an adequate theoretical treatment of the problem, and if his theory could be restated in such fashion as to eliminate the confusion to which we have just directed attention, it might prove useful in the extreme.

former distinctly preferable. But he does not say this; and since he adds that where the members have "expressly agreed in any number greater than the majority,"[18] that arrangement also is legitimate, it may well be that he does not intend even to imply it. (To stipulate in favor of decision-making by extraordinary majority is, obviously, to stipulate in favor of a *minority-right* to conclude the majority.) In short, the single clear implication of the statement, as it stands, is that any sort of government to which men have at some time consented is lawful, and the safest conclusions seem to be (a) that the *Second Treatise* contains no unequivocal doctrine on this point, and (b) that the passage in question was intended merely as a reiteration of his general doctrine of consent as the basis of lawful government, its apparent emphasis upon majority-right being the result of careless wording.

Fourth Argument. Political bodies, like all other bodies, must move in the direction in which they are impelled by the greater force, and in political bodies the greater force is the will of the majority.

This we may call the argument by analogy, and, like the argument from necessity, it has attracted many subsequent writers. What it amounts to is an insistence that majority-determination in political societies is natural, as it is natural for water to seek its level, for the heavier end of a seesaw to point downward, and (to follow the direction which Krabbe gives to the argument) for the human mind to make that decision to which it is drawn by the more weighty reasons. Its inarticulate major premise, when urged as an argument in favor of the right of the majority, is that the natural is not only natural but also right.

In Locke's hands the argument consists of the following steps: The motivating force of a community, in virtue of which alone it can act as a community, is the consent (past promise? present support?) of its individual members. Therefore the greater motivating force within it is the consent of the greater number of its individual members, and, at the limit, the consent of one half of those members plus one. If, then, we were to suppose it capable of responding to the force exerted by the smaller number of its individual members, we should have to suppose it different in this respect from all other bodies of which we possess knowledge.[19]

The argument is intensely interesting, if only as a reminder of the justice of Professor Catlin's acknowledgment of indebtedness to the contract theorists;[20] for here, in a paragraph, is the central conception of his

---

[18] viii. 99.
[19] viii. 96. The language in the text is a free but (the writer believes) faithful paraphrase.
[20] Catlin, *Principles*, p. 169: "Men will become, not fugitive from society, but rebels against it, unless they are permitted to believe that they are acting freely in those things to which they attach most value. Restraint has no theoretical limit, but constraint can be imposed by no prudent statesman without a cautious calculation of his power to enforce it. *The theorists of the seventeenth and eighteenth centuries were, then, quite right in founding the contract upon the possibility of a rebellious attitude of will in every man.* It is not possible to quit society; but it is very possible to be anti-social, and, still more, anti-national, anti-group, impious, unconventional" (italics mine).

admirable *Principles of Politics*. Those familiar with the refinement it has received in Professor Catlin's treatment will, therefore, see at once that it owes its plausibility (in Locke) to a carefully concealed *non sequitur*. The argument is unexceptionable insofar as it asserts that the motivating force of a community is consent—*if* we understand by consent present support rather than past commitment. It is unexceptionable, again, insofar as it asserts that the consent which motivates a community is a consent given (ultimately) by individuals. It is unexceptionable, finally, insofar as it asserts that more consent (for consent *is* additive) generates a greater motivating force than less consent. But it does not follow from these propositions that the consent which motivates a given society at any given moment is that of the greater number of its individual members, unless we are in a position to assume that the members are equally active in giving and withholding their consent, and unless, further, we are in a position to assume that the consents given and withheld are of equal *intensity*.[21] No spectacle is more familiar in politics than that of a majority's abdication of responsibility for the making of decisions, unless it be that of the ease with which a smaller number of persons with intense convictions can make their consent count for more than that of a larger number of persons who, without joining the politically inactive majority, are yet not prepared, on the particular issue at stake, to offer resistance to the smaller number. The validity of Locke's conclusion rests, therefore, on two hidden premises (equal individual participation in the making of decisions, equal intensity of conviction on each issue to be decided) of whose necessity he reveals no sort of awareness; and we must conclude that that which he declares to be natural is natural only where certain indispensable conditions are satisfied.

If, *per impossibile*, we were to waive these objections, and grant for argument's sake that decisions by majority-vote are a natural phenomenon of community life, there would remain the difficulty that we cannot argue from the naturalness of the process by which the majority concludes the minority to a *majority-right* to conclude the minority—or, if the reader prefers, we cannot argue from the one to the other without first demonstrating our title to do so.

Fifth Argument. Individual consents being, in any case, the only rightful title to the exercise of power, the right of the majority flows as a matter of course from the fact that it can point to more consents than the minority.

This, in the opinion of the present writer, is what was really in Locke's mind as he wrote the paragraphs in which he attempts to defend the notion of majority-right, although, admittedly, some exegesis is needed

---

[21] Cf. *ibid.*, p. 266: "If all men were equal, or if government were only possible if all men believed themselves to have an equal share, then only majority government (over-riding the 'equal shares' of the minority as a practical expedient) would be feasible."

in order to establish its presence in those paragraphs. A man, the argument runs, necessarily surrenders some of his liberty when he subscribes to the compact which makes him a member of a commonwealth.[22] The compact "would signify nothing, and be no compact if he be left free and under no other ties than he was in before in the state of Nature. . . . What new engagement [would there be] if he were no farther tied by any decrees of the society than *he himself thought* fit and did actually consent to?"[23] In consenting to be a member of a commonwealth, therefore, he consents beforehand to the acceptance of obligations which he does not himself approve, and it is right that he should do so because such an obligation is implicit in the nature of community life. And the character of the obligation, be it noted, is to be discovered in a situation in which the community, otherwise unanimous (as we are clearly asked to conceive it in the passage cited), is making a demand of the individual to which he is not prepared to give his consent. The compact would be all to the advantage of the individual, thus no compact, if it did not involve a duty on the part of the individual to fulfill the demand, thus also a right on the part of the community to make it, thus also a reciprocal obligation among all the individuals in the community to fulfill such a demand when it happens to be made of them. In other words, that community life to which all the individuals consent is possible on no other basis; and therefore, Locke is saying, "every man, by consenting with others to make one body politic under one government, puts himself under an obligation to every one of that society to submit to the determination of the majority."[24]

Now the thing which Locke's critics have failed to perceive (thus overlooking the major emphasis of his defense of the majority-principle) is that, although he does not assist us with the deduction, the right of the majority to conclude the minority does follow as a matter of course from the right of the community to conclude the individual, *insofar as that right is defended in terms of the community's numerical superiority over the individual.* If one million persons have a right to conclude one because they are a million and he is only one, then there is no logical escape from the conclusion that five hundred thousand and one persons have a right to conclude five hundred thousand persons, and if one does not like the conclusion one must revise one's notions regarding the premise.

In a word, Locke had apprehended—on a half-conscious level—a tremendously important logical relation between the doctrine that the whole people have a right to have their way and the doctrine that the majority have a right to have their way. For either you mean, by the former doctrine, that the people must be really unanimous in order to exert their rightful authority, in which case there will be no one left upon whom it can be exerted, or you mean, as we have gone to some pains to show that Locke always did, that virtual unanimity is as good a title to authority as the people require, in which case you must be willing (as Locke was) to go ahead and defend—without any of those "subterfuges" to which Professor Friedrich refers—the majority-principle.

We conclude: (a) that the first, second, third, and fourth of these arguments in favor of majority-right may properly be dismissed as unworthy of serious consideration; (b) that, insofar as he intended to show with his fourth argument that his theory of majority-right is logically implied in his theory of popular sovereignty, he was on safe ground; and (c) that our evaluation of his theory of majority-right must be dictated by our evaluation of his theory of popular sovereignty.

CHAPTER VIII

POLITICAL EQUALITY

THE EXTENT of Locke's verbal commitment to the position of the majority-rule democrats of our own day with respect to political equality may be inferred from the passages analyzed in the preceding chapter. As we have pointed out in our Introduction, to claim power for the majority of the individual members of a society is, *ceteris paribus*, to declare those individual members political equals, since it is to claim for each one the power to cast the deciding vote in virtue of which, at the limit, the majority *is* a majority—or since (to put the same thing in another way) it is to claim for each, before every decision, an equal capacity to affect the result of the ballot.[1] And, since Locke certainly makes the former claim, he may fairly be said to have committed himself (verbally) to the latter.[2] Broadly speaking, therefore, we may say of his theory of equality that it is involved in his theory of the majority-principle, as, in the preceding chapter, we have shown his theory of the majority-principle to be involved in his theory of popular sovereignty; thus, also, that the three theories really constitute a *single* theory with three emphases which, for purposes of convenience, we have chosen to consider separately; thus, finally, that the three theories stand or fall together. This commentary upon Locke's theory of equality must, however, be read against the background of the following considerations:

(a) Because of the wide divergence between Locke's position and that of the majority-rule democrats of our own day with respect to the problem dealt with in the following chapter, his theory of equality admits of the possibility of vast political inequality over what (borrowing a phrase from the economists) we may call the "short period" (*i.e.*, the period between revolutions).

(b) It is a matter of some interest (in the light of what we have said in our Introduction regarding the advisability of keeping political problems separate in our minds from economic and social problems) that the equality Locke claims for the members of his society is *political* in the strictest sense of the word. Unlike many of the majority-rule democrats of our own day, and unlike Rousseau,[3] Locke was not prepared to dictate

---

[1]Cf. Aaron, *op. cit.*, p. 273: "For Locke . . . . a political community is an organization of equals . . . . into which men enter voluntarily in order to achieve together what they cannot achieve apart."
[2]Cf. Alfred Tuttle Williams, *The Concept of Equality in the Writings of Rousseau, Bentham and Kant* (New York: Teachers' College, Columbia University, 1907), p. 10: "The dictum that 'men are by nature free and equal,' which was accepted by the American Fathers as a self-evident proposition, may be traced immediately to Locke."
[3]Cf. Rousseau, *op. cit.*, ii. 11, where he argues that without equality "la liberté ne peut subsister," and adds, "Quant à la richesse, que nul citoyen ne soit assez opulent pour en pouvoir acheter un autre, et nul assez pauvre pour être contraint de se vendre."

to the members of his commonwealth the principles of economic distribution which they must adopt, or to insist that men must be equal in all things in order to enjoy an equal voice in the making of laws. He explains at one point in the *Second Treatise*:

> Though I have said above "That all men by nature are equal," I cannot be supposed to understand all sorts of "equality." Age or virtue may give men a just precedency. Excellency of parts and merit may place others above the common level. Birth may subject some, and alliance or benefits others, to pay an observance to those to whom Nature, gratitude, or other respects, may have made it due; and yet all this consists with . . . . that equal right that every man hath to his natural freedom, without being subjected to the will or authority of any other man.[4]

(c) While lunatics, idiots, children, and (temporary) madmen are the only classes which he expressly excludes from the (equal) rights which attach to membership in his commonwealth,[5] it seems highly improbable that Locke was thinking in terms of extending those rights to women. Officially, his doctrine is that "we are born free [= equally free = equal] as we are born rational,"[6] a proposition of which much might be made in connection with a determined effort to enlist his support for the movement for woman suffrage; and the same thing may be said of his vigorous denunciation of Filmer for having overlooked the claims of mothers when he sought to rest the case for monarchy on the rights attaching to fatherhood.[7] But the following passage suggests that Locke's notions on the position of women were those of his age, thus that the "people" (thus also the majority) for whom he claimed power was a

[4] vi. 54.

[5] vi. 60. Cf. Wilson, *op. cit.*, p. 120: "We must not forget . . . . that neither Locke nor his follower Jefferson were democrats in the modern sense of the word, for neither believed in either universal or manhood suffrage." Cf. MacIver, *Leviathan*, p. 92: "The leaders of the [American] Revolution accepted the principle that the people were the locus of sovereignty, but the people were conceived in the *Lockian* sense. They were the substantial folk as distinguished from the rabble" (italics mine). Cf. Lamprecht, *op. cit.*, p. 140 n.: "To what extent Locke would wish to give political power to all classes of the population is uncertain. Even the Republicans like Milton and Harrington opposed universal suffrage, and would grant the ballot only to the competent or land-owning classes . . . . Whether Locke followed these predecessors . . . . is difficult to determine. *His discussion of majority rule and the consent of the governed seems to point to a more broadly democratic point of view*; but if the general assumptions of his generation are considered, his failure to state explicitly that he favored universally shared political power can almost [!] be interpreted as satisfaction with the quite limited democracy of the English constitution in his day" (italics mine). Professor Lamprecht's admirable scholarly caution makes it difficult to say whether or not he would take issue with the point made in the text, where we are concerned less with what Locke thought in his heart of hearts (interesting as that would be to know) than with what Locke said in the *Second Treatise*. If Lamprecht had said that the discussion of majority-rule and the consent of the governed actually points to a more broadly democratic point of view (instead of only seeming to), or if he had said that we are entitled to attribute to Locke the general assumptions of his generation insofar as he does not expressly dissociate himself from them (instead of "almost"), we might safely observe that the latter point is doubtful and that, in any case, Locke *is* explicit about majority-rule and the consent of the governed (as Professor Lamprecht almost admits) and thus stands committed to that which (manhood suffrage) is implied in his treatment of them. Not, to be sure, manhood suffrage in elections held at regular intervals, but an equal right in every man to consent or refuse to form a part of a contemplated revolutionary majority. As for suffrage in parliamentary elections, where a majority of the society has decreed them, we have pointed out in the text that Locke's principles admit of political inequality in the short period. For the rest, men have been hanged for less explicit pronouncements upon the subject of political equality than the following words, hidden in Locke's account of the state of nature (ii. 4): "There . . . . [is] nothing more evident than that creatures of the same species and rank, promiscuously born to all the same advantages of Nature, and the use of the same faculties, *should also be equal one amongst another, without subordination or subjection*, unless the lord and master of them all should, by any manifest declaration of his will, set one above another, and confer on him . . . . an undoubted right to dominion and sovereignty" (italics mine). Note the final word of the quotation, and cf. Lamprecht's statement ("Hobbes and Hobbism," *loc. cit.*) that Locke could compose an entire treatise on government without mentioning it.

[6] vi. 61. Cf. vi. 59, where he directs attention to the "supposition" in English law that rationality begins at the age of twenty-one, and offers no objection.

[7] vi. 53.

more restricted group than that which figures in the thinking of many more recent majority-rule democrats:

The husband and wife, though they have but one common concern, yet having different understandings, will unavoidably sometimes have different wills too. It therefore being necessary that the last determination (*i.e.*, the rule) should be placed somewhere, it naturally falls to the man's share as the abler and stronger.[8]

(d) Locke was apparently no more aware than the majority-rule democrats of our day of the considerations which make it necessary for *us* to write the reservation *ceteris paribus* into the proposition that the making of political decisions by majority-vote is compatible with (even formal) political equality. It is easy to see—once the problem has forced itself upon one's mind—that, in (*e.g.*) a group in which a "crystallized" majority (made up of persons who, whether out of conviction or out of self-interest or, what is perhaps more usual, a little of each, vote together on all issues) has arrogated to itself the function of making group decisions, a group in which the member of the minority knows, before deliberation takes place, that he is *not* in position to affect the result of the ballot, compliance with the majority-principle entails, for the minority, any degree of political subjection which the majority cares to impose upon them.[9] It is easy to see, again, that if with the passing of time the crystallized majority learns (as modern political parties have learned) to entrust to a majority of its own members the power to conclude the minority of its own members, fidelity to the majority-principle can come to involve political subjection for the *majority* of the members of the wider group.[10] It was this order of considerations which led Starosolskyj to limit his argument for the majority-principle to situations characterized by what he calls "indeterminacy of the relations of subordination and superordination,"[11] and which led Rousseau (to whom Starosolskyj does not express his indebtedness) to place so much emphasis upon (a) the prohibition of "partial" organizations within the political society,[12] and (b) the impossibility of eliciting a "general will" where many votes are cast by persons who place self-interest before the general interest.[13] Locke, we repeat, saw nothing of all this—a failure which is, in this writer's opinion, intimately related to the vagueness of his statements regarding the character of that "public good" to the promotion of which he represents his political society as dedicated. Here, as elsewhere, his central difficulty is the cavalier unconcern with which he (by implication) extends to existing commonwealths propositions which

---

[8]vii. 82.
[9]Cf. Jellinek, *op. cit.*, p. 41.
[10]Indeed, for all the members of the group except the two members who constitute a majority of the triad in which, if such a process were continued indefinitely, decision-making power would finally rest. The writer is indebted for this suggestion to Professor John A. Fairlie.
[11]Cf. Starosolskyj, *op. cit.*, p. 65, p. 89.
[12]Rousseau, *op. cit.*, ii. 3.
[13]*Ibid.*

(as he should have seen) apply only to situations in which the phrase "the public good" can be filled up with meaning.

(e) While the existence of a public good which men are prepared to place above their selfish interests is a *necessary* condition for the compatibility of majority-decisions and political equality (*i.e.*, where no such good exists there seems to be no reason to expect for the minority any result other than political subjection), it must be noticed that, conceptually, the notion of a public good which is both public and *good* is not easy to reconcile with that of political equality. If, that is to say, we insist (with Locke at his best) that claims to rights must be granted or denied according as the rights claimed are or are not compatible with the public good, then we are logically committed either to the view that equal political rights are appropriate only to those situations in which men possess equal capacity and equal willingness to use their power (to affect decisions) in the general interest, or to the admission that Locke's political system presupposes not merely the existence of a public good, but the existence of a public good of a very special kind—*i.e.*, one which *by definition* ceases to be good unless achieved upon a cooperative and egalitarian basis. That it is such a good which the majority-rule democrats have in mind when they condemn as incompatible with the general interest any principle other than that of equality and decisions by majority-vote is a thing which becomes increasingly evident to the student of their thought, but one which none of them (except possibly Marx) has defined with any degree of precision.[14]

---

[14]It is interesting to note that this implication concerning the special nature of the public good in a democracy did not entirely escape notice in the ancient world. The Old Oligarch, in his ironic defence of the Athenian polity, argues that rule by the people must be considered as a good *per se*, for one is, he says, obliged to concede that the government best for the state would be a government administered by the most capable men and would thus necessarily deprive the many of participation in the making of decisions (Pseudo-Xenophon, *Constitution of Athens*, i. 8-9).

CHAPTER IX

THE PROBLEM OF POPULAR CONSULTATION

WE HAVE SAID that Locke's solution for the basic problems of politics is at all points *save one* that of the majority-rule democrats. The exception is to be found in those of his opinions which relate to what we are today accustomed to call the problem of popular consultation; and the position is, briefly, that he virtually ignores the necessity (an apparently inescapable corollary of his doctrine regarding popular sovereignty and his doctrine regarding majority-decisions) for political *machinery* by means of which the popular (or majority) will may express itself. In that section of his book which comes most readily to mind in this connection, we find Locke arguing, *in effect,* as follows:

I have already demonstrated that the only lawful title to the exercise of political power is popular consent. I have already demonstrated, too, that the majority of the people have a right to speak, in this matter of consent, for the whole people. I have, in fact, gone so far as to argue that it is unnatural, thus wrong, for the body politic to move in any direction except that in which it is carried by the greater (= the majority's) consent. Now, what does this mean with regard to the day-to-day conduct of the affairs of a political society? Simply this: that any scheme for making and enforcing laws whose defenders can point to authorization by a popular majority at some time in the past is the right scheme for the political society in question until it is altered by the mandate of a popular majority. That is, the majority, at any moment when it is active, may make what arrangements it pleases for the future governance of its society; and those arrangements then possess the highest sanction which can be claimed for a scheme of government.

The above, it is suggested, is not an unfair statement (for all that it says nothing of natural rights and impartial judges) of the implications of the majoritarian *défi* which Locke wrote into his chapter "Of the Forms of a Commonwealth."

The majority . . . . may . . . . [make] laws for the community from time to time, and . . . . [execute] those laws by officers of their own appointing, and then the form of the government is a perfect democracy; or else may put the power of making laws into the hands of a few select men, and their heirs or successors, and then it is an oligarchy; or else into the hands of one man, and then it is a monarchy. . . . And so accordingly of these make compounded and mixed forms of government, *as they think good.*[1]

The majority may, if it likes, set up an *hereditary* monarchy, and name the period for which it is to continue in the exercise of legislative power! The majority may, if it chooses, act to prevent the exercise of power by future majorities![2]

---

[1] x. 132 (italics mine).
[2] *Ibid.* Cf. Carpenter, *op. cit.,* p. 103: "[The sovereignty of the community in Locke's political philosophy] is compatible with almost any variety of institutions, so long as it is recognized that the rulers are the trustees of the people who delegate their power to them."

How very different from this is the attitude of the majority-rule democrats of our day will be evident to the most casual student of their writings. J. Allen Smith, in his vigorous indictment of the government of the United States, is not really raising the question, Can (*e.g.*) the supporters of judicial review point to that occasion, in American history, when the majority of the American people expressed a preference for that method of constitutional interpretation?—despite his manifest conviction that the constitution was written (and, in a manner of speaking, imposed upon the American people) by a minority of property owners. Smith's real grievance, throughout, is against those aspects of the constitution which, on the one hand, make it difficult for *present* majorities to express their will, and, on the other hand, restrict their power to make that will effective. Any constitutional device which can be shown to have either of these effects is objectionable to him, and for that reason. Herman Finer's *Theory and Practice of Modern Government,* again, although avowedly an *apologia* for the majority-rule emphases of the British constitution, is by no means a demonstration that British government is (in some sense in which American, French, and German government are not) the *handiwork* of a popular majority, but rather that in Great Britain there exists from *moment to moment* (as in the United States, France, and Germany there does not) a presumption that what government does is done with the *approval* of a popular majority.[3]

Now it is a matter of some interest (as Professor Friedrich[4] and others, who would like to charge the majority-rule democrats with responsibility for the Hitler régime in Germany, are fond of pointing out) that the former attitude (*i.e.,* Locke's) is apparently *more* consistent with the plea for the lodgment of unrestricted political power in the hands of popular majorities than the latter attitude (*i.e.,* that of Smith and Finer). How, it seems natural to inquire, can we speak of an unlimited right in the majority to make decisions binding upon the minority if, in the next breath, we are to demand that it respect the right of tomorrow's majority and next year's? If what the majority decrees is right because the majority decrees it, why should not this be equally true of what the majority decrees regarding the future governance of the society? And if the majority's decrees regarding the future governance of the society are *not* equally sacred with its other decrees, if there is some better method by which we can arrive at decisions regarding governmental forms, why not employ that same method for all other decisions? Locke, on such a showing, is merely facing the unavoidable implications

---

[3]Although Professor Finer, in a conversation with the writer in the Spring of 1938, expressed strong opposition to the notion of setting up in Great Britain any machinery for popular recall of governments.

[4]Friedrich, "One Majority Against Another," *passim.*

of the assertions which we have examined in our chapter on the right of the majority.

The consistency of such a view with the notion of majority-right is, however, apparent only; and Locke cannot be too severely condemned for having stumbled so blindly into a trap which his good sense (to say nothing of his democratic instincts) should have enabled him to avoid. The following considerations seem worth urging in this connection:

(a) To assert, or prove, that (to use Locke's own phrase) the majority have a right to conclude the rest, is merely to assert (or prove) that when—in a situation where sovereignty is understood to inhere in the people—a majority favors one policy and a minority another, the latter should accommodate itself to the former. To seek to read out of the proposition the implication that today's majority may by fiat suppress the right upon which its own decrees depend for what validity they possess is to ignore the fact that the proposition as stated attributes to the majority a *continuous* right, and that the implication in question can be extracted from it only by ignoring a part of its clear signification. If, again, the proposition "the majority have a right to conclude the rest" implies that the majority have a right to withdraw the right of the majority, then it implies its own contradictory, is not a valid proposition, and had best be abandoned as a criterion of political right. If, again, the proposition that the majority have a right to conclude the rest can be made to mean that the majority have a right to set up an hereditary monarchy (or any other kind!), it implies that the majority have a right to suspend that right of the whole people from which (in Locke's hands) its own right derives!

(b) To suppose that the right of the majority includes the right to suspend majority-rule is to take for granted the proposition that the possessor of a right has, as a matter of course, the right to bestow it elsewhere. Now, while there are undoubtedly *legal* rights of this character (*e.g.,* the ownership of some forms of property), it is by no means clear that we can conceive of a moral right of this character, since to assert such a thing with respect to a moral right is to forget the axiom, to which we have often alluded in the foregoing pages, that A's right is merely B's duty regarded from another point of view. The right of the majority to conclude the minority, that is to say, is (at most) merely the correlate of the minority's duty to be concluded by the majority; and while it may seem easy to argue from the majority's right to conclude the minority to its right to bestow that right elsewhere, the conclusion can be accepted only if it be shown that the minority has a duty to be concluded by those upon whom the majority bestows the right. Locke was, therefore, quite right in making of his defense of the majority-principle an attempted demonstration that the minority ought to obey the majority;

but for that reason he should have seen that the arguments he employs in that demonstration in fact exclude a duty of obedience to any decrees *save* those of the majority (or its indisputable agent).

(c) While Locke may properly be chided for his failure to see that his theory of governmental forms was inconsistent with his statement of the majority-principle, it is only fair to notice that that failure is intimately related to other weaknesses in his political theory. As we have intimated elsewhere, many of Locke's difficulties flow from his infidelity to the axiom (of which he has shown, at times, a clear grasp) that rights lapse when the person or persons in whom they inhere fail to discharge the duties which attach to them.[5] Locke's difficulties, that is to say, often flow from his initial error of asking *what persons* have the right of making laws—a question which leads easily to the further question, Does the majority have that right? This is the question to which his majority-principle is, clearly, an answer; and, having once received it as a proper question (*i.e.,* not a *question mal posée*), having once assumed the responsibility of answering it in the affirmative without first criticizing it, he has put by the controls which might have saved him from the blunder to which we direct attention in the present chapter. If he had, *ab initio,* clung fast to the notion that the right of the majority is a function of its duties, as on his own principles he should have, he would have recognized the absurdity of the doctrine that the right of the majority to make decisions for the society is valid even at the moment when it is abdicating its *duties* by transferring decision-making power to other persons.

Our criticism of this branch of Locke's theory is, then, that having overlooked the *inherent* limitations upon the power of the majority involved in the notion of majority-right, he permitted himself to neglect the difficult question of how to make law and government continuously responsible to the will of the majority. We say "neglect" (as above, we have said "almost completely ignored") because that right of revolution which, under the compact, vests continuously in the majority, is clearly an attempt—a tardy and unsuccessful attempt—to deal with the difficulty here under consideration.

Now there are two possible interpretations of what Locke says about the right of revolution. Those who see a kind of *contract* in the relation between people and government in Locke's system are apparently committed to the view that the right of revolution can be exercised only when the government has violated the agreement between itself and the majority from which it received its grant of legislative and executive

---

[5]As others flow from the fact that he never made up his mind whether government by consent means government by *previous* popular authorization or government with continuous popular approval—a confusion which reveals itself even in his initial discussion of the law of nature. In order to avoid it he would have needed to work out a formula including *both* the fifth and sixth theses.

power—*i.e.*, that today's majority can regard itself as free to dissolve the government established by yesterday's majority only when that government has *really failed* to carry out the intentions of yesterday's majority. That interpretation has the advantage of reconciling the right of revolution with the position enunciated in the passage quoted at the beginning of the present chapter and (while we have already stated at some length our reasons for repudiating it) therefore it should not be overlooked in the present connection. Obviously, however, it accomplishes the reconciliation only at the cost of involving Locke still more deeply in the difficulty elaborated in the above paragraphs, namely, that of using the doctrine of majority-rule to legitimate, on occasion, the exercise of political power by a minority.

On the second interpretation, our own, Locke intended the majority to exercise its right of revolution at its own discretion, intended that the government of his political society *should* be continuously responsive to the will of the majority, intended the chapter "Of the Forms of a Commonwealth" to be read against the background of the dictum, "the legislative being only a fiduciary power to act for certain ends, there remains still in the people [thus in the majority] a *supreme* power to remove or alter the legislative,"[6] and supposed that an understanding to the effect that the majority possesses such a right of revolution would be an adequate guarantee that government *will* be subservient to the majority-will.

Since it seems improbable that Locke was thinking here in any terms so modern as Professor Friedrich's "law of anticipated reactions,"[7] in terms, that is to say, of a more or less automatic adjustment of the governmental act to the popular will brought about by the government's concern to avoid a revolution, he must have supposed (1) that independently of institutional midwifery of any kind, there will at all moments exist such a thing as a majority-will with which governmental law and policy can be made to coincide, (2) that the majority will in fact revolt when the governmental act does not coincide with its will, and (3) that revolutionary movements enjoying majority support can be counted upon to succeed.

Now all three of these propositions call for acts of faith of which few students of the history of democratic government during the past two centuries will find themselves capable. Because they do not believe that revolutionary movements enjoying popular support necessarily succeed, the majority-rule democrats of our day insist upon institutions calculated to avoid the necessity for making them (periodic elections, prompt removal of legislators and executive officials unable to elicit votes

---

[6] xiii. 149 (italics mine).
[7] Cf. Friedrich, *Constitutional Government and Politics*, p. 16. But cf. xiv. 168: "This [majority dissatisfaction with the government] the executive power, or wise princes, never need come in the danger of; and it is the thing of all others they have most need to avoid, as, of all others, the most perilous."

of confidence in those elections, *etc.*, which secure the same results by "peaceful" means), and institutions calculated to discourage governments from creating situations in which a revolution could not succeed (small standing armies, subservience of military to civil officials, *etc.*). Because they do not believe that the majority can be counted on to rebel when it finds its will thwarted, they attach all the more importance to institutions calculated to make the majority-will, as expressed in elections, equally effective with the majority-will as expressed through a successful revolution. And because they do not believe that the people can be counted upon to produce a majority-will except where certain conditions are satisfied, they insist upon institutions calculated to facilitate the emergence of such a will (popular education, ventilation of public issues before the widest possible audience and with fullest guarantees that all points of view will find expression, such freedom of organization for political parties as will assure a maximum of competition between them for majority support, *etc.*). In short, they restate Locke's right of revolution in terms of a popular right to be consulted about governmental affairs at regular intervals (the proper length of the intervals being a matter about which there is much difference of opinion among them), and to be consulted in such a way as to marshal a well-informed majority behind *some* policy whose proponents have been obliged to defend it against vigorous criticism. On either showing, therefore, Locke's treatment of the right of revolution is a fatal weakness in his theory.

It is interesting to notice that these three propositions about majorities (of which we have not intended, thus far, to say more than that they are *logically* involved in his theory) are things which Locke actually believed at the time he wrote the *Second Treatise*: "Nor let any one think," he says in defending the right of revolution, "this lays a perpetual foundation for disorder; for this operates not till the inconvenience is so great that the majority feel it, and are weary of it, and find a necessity to have it amended";[8] *i.e.*, when the inconvenience *is* great, a majority opinion to that effect spontaneously takes shape. Nor does the inconvenience need to be the present inconvenience of the members of the majority themselves; they are alert to abuses suffered by minorities, where these presage future dangers for the society as a whole, and they may be counted upon to rebel when such abuses occur!

If . . . . [the] illegal acts have extended to the majority of the people, or if the mischief and oppression has light only on some few, but in such cases as the precedent and consequences seem to threaten all, and they are persuaded in their consciences that their laws, and with them, their estates, liberties, and lives are in danger, and perhaps their religion too, how they will be hindered from resisting illegal force used against them I cannot tell.[9]

[8]xiv. 168.
[9]xviii. 209.

History shows, finally, that their resistance will be successful:

The people generally ill treated, and contrary to right, will be ready upon any occasion to ease themselves of a burden that sits heavy upon them. They will wish and seek for the opportunity, which in the change, weakness, and accidents of human affairs, *seldom delays long to offer itself*. He must have lived but a little while in the world, who has not seen examples of this in his time; and he must have read very little who cannot produce examples of it in all sorts of governments in the world.[10]

Small wonder, then, that Locke felt himself under no obligation to work out for his readers techniques for forming and laying bare the will of the majority.[11] They are not needed!

Thomas Hill Green, to whose discussion of Locke we have already had occasion to refer, brings against Locke's right of revolution an objection which, though of an essentially different character from those urged here, nevertheless adds further weight to our conclusion that Locke should have given attention to the problem of implementing the right with appropriate institutions. How, he demands of Locke, except in such a special situation as that which obtains in a Swiss canton, is anyone ever to be sure that a successful revolution has not had the effect of removing a government satisfactory to the majority?

Any sectary or revolutionary may plead that he has the sovereign people on his side. If he fails, it is not certain that he has them not on his side; for it may be that, though he has the majority of the society on his side, yet the society has allowed the growth within it of a power which prevents it from giving effect to its will. On the other hand, if the revolution succeeds, it is not certain that it had the majority on its side when it began, though the majority may have come to acquiesce in the result.[12]

---

[10]xix. 224 (italics mine).

[11]Admirers of Locke may well protest that this is unfair, since it does not take account of such brilliant insights as the following: (a) "The people having reserved to themselves the choice of their representatives as the fence to their properties, could do it for no other end but that they might always be *freely* chosen, and so chosen, freely *act and advise as the necessity of the commonwealth and the public good should, upon examination and mature debate, be judged to require*. This, those who give their votes before they hear the debate, and have weighed the reasons on all sides, are not capable of doing" (xix. 222, italics mine). (b) "Whenever the people shall choose their representatives upon just and undeniably equal measures, ... it cannot be doubted to be the will and act of the society, whoever permitted or proposed to them to do so" (xiii. 158)—wherefore the king may without legal authorization reapportion seats in parliament upon a basis of "true reason" (*ibid.*). (c) "It is a mistake to think that the supreme or legislative power of any commonwealth can do what it will, and dispose of the estates of the subject arbitrarily, or take any part of them at pleasure. This is not much to be feared in governments where the legislative consists wholly or in part in assemblies which are variable, whose members upon the dissolution of the assembly are subjects under the common laws of their country, equally with the rest" (xi. 138). (d) "In well-ordered commonwealths, where the good of the whole is so considered as it ought, the legislative power is put into the hands of divers persons who, duly assembled, have by themselves, or jointly with others, a power to make laws, which when they have done, being separated again, they are themselves subject to the laws they have made; which is a new and near tie upon them to take care that they make them for the public good" (xii. 143). Of these, (c) and (d) clearly imply that an institutional device calculated to prevent "particular" legislation is a good thing whether the majority have ordered it or not; (a) clearly recognizes the need for free and full discussion in the elaboration of governmental policy; and (b) appears in the course of an argument which clearly takes for granted the desirability of representation apportioned to population. But the reference of (a) is to the legislative, not the populace, (b) is followed by the reservation that the reapportionment must be suitable to the "original frame of the government" (*i.e.*, the intentions of that majority which set it up), and (c) and (d) do not really face the institutional problem to which they are directed.

[12]Green, *op. cit.*, p. 77. Cf. xviii. 208: "It [is] . . . . as impossible for one or a few oppressed men to disturb the government where the body of the people do not think themselves concerned in it, as for a raving madman or heady malcontent to overturn a well-settled state, the people being as little apt to follow the one as the other."

Green concludes that Locke should have abandoned his majoritarian doctrine altogether, and recognized that it is not majority support but "the function which it serves in maintaining those conditions of freedom which are conditions of the moral life" which gives a government its title to obedience;[13] but the majority-rule democrat of our day can reply that in a nation in which, as is modern England, there exists a vigorous and healthy competition between freely organized political parties, an electoral system so devised as to justify a presumption that electoral majorities are popular majorities, and institutional guarantees that elections will be held at regular intervals, his criticism is beside the point. We do know, in such a background, what sectary has the majority of the people on his side; and the logical corollary of Locke's doctrine of majority-rule is a demand for an institutional context in which the people are as a matter of course invited, from time to time, to express (by majority-vote) their preferences regarding future government policy and personnel.

---

[13]*Ibid.*, p. 78.

CHAPTER X

THE LATENT PREMISE

Quand une société ou sa majorité veut une chose, elle est juste.
Celui qui s'y oppose, qui appelle la vengeance sur la nation, est un
monstre. L'ordre se trouve toujours dans l'accord de la majorité.
*La minorité est toujours coupable, je le répète, eût-elle raison
moralement; il ne faut que du sens commun pour sentir cette
vérité là.*[1]

THE MAJOR CONCLUSION which the writer would like to rest upon the
evidence considered in the present study is that the above lines might well
have been written by someone who had taken the John Locke of the
Second Treatise as his mentor in political philosophy. The attitude which
they express towards majority-rule *is* that of the *Second Treatise*, and the
prevailing impression to the contrary must be set down as an illustration
of what happens when scholars abdicate responsibility for reading the
books which they criticize. Locke can, to be sure, be quoted as saying that
"where the body of the people, *or any single man,* are deprived of their
right, or are under the exercise of a power without right, ... they
have a liberty to appeal to Heaven whenever they judge the cause of
sufficient moment,"[2] and we have so quoted him. He can be quoted (and
has been quoted) as saying that the right to judge whether or not to
appeal to Heaven is something which the individual cannot part with,
since it is "out of a man's power so to submit himself to another [or
others] as to give him a liberty to destroy him."[3] But it is in this same
passage that he says that the principle in question "operates not till the
inconvenience be so great that the majority . . . . find a necessity to have
it amended"! And it is only a few pages later that he *defends* the people's
(= the majority's) right of revolution in terms of the fact that "the
examples of particular injustice or oppression of here and there an
unfortunate man moves them not."[4]

---

[1]Restif de la Bretonne, *ap.* Saripolos, *op. cit.,* p. 256. Cf. Story, *op. cit.,* I, pp. 220-221: "The
truth is that the majority of every organized society have always claimed, and exercised the
right to govern the whole of that society, in the manner pointed out by the fundamental laws,
which from time to time have existed in such society. Every revolution, at least when not pro-
duced by positive force, has been founded upon the authority of such majority. And the right
results from the very necessities of our nature; for universal consent can never be practically
required or obtained. *The minority are bound, whether they have assented or not;* for the plain
reason, that opposite wills in the same society, on the same subjects, cannot prevail at the same
time; and, as society is instituted for the general safety and happiness, in a conflict of opinion *the
majority must have a right to accomplish that object by the means which they deem adequate for
the end.* The majority may, indeed, decide how far they will respect the rights or claims of the
minority, and how far they will, from policy or principle, insist upon or absolve them from
obedience. But this is a matter, on which they decide for themselves, according to their own
notions of justice or convenience. In a general sense the will of the majority of the people
is absolute and sovereign, limited only by their means and power to make their will effective."
(italics mine). Story was not always willing to go so far with the majority-rule democrats. Cf.
ibid., I, pp. 372-373, 376, 393; II, p. 325.
[2]xiv. 168 (italics mine).
[3]*Ibid.*
[4]xix. 230. On Rousseau's showing, such injustice or oppression would terminate the compact.

How are we to explain to ourselves this man who tells us, in a single paragraph, that the individual has a right to appeal to Heaven when he judges the cause sufficient, and must not do so until the majority is ready to join him in that appeal? Did Locke really mean that the majority has a right to (*e.g.*) maintain in power a government which oppresses or treats unjustly the "rest"? Did he really believe that it is the fact of majority support which *makes* right in politics? The correct reply to these questions is: Obviously not; Locke could never have committed himself to the moral relativism implied in the proposition that majorities make right—as anyone can see from reading the first three pages of the *Second Treatise*. Here is a writer who believed, with a passion which has rarely been equalled in the history of political theory, not only in the moral law but also in the possibility of applying the moral law to the problems of politics!

What, then, is the key to the riddle of the *Second Treatise?* It is, in the opinion of the present writer, to be found in the fact that, while the proposition "right is that which the majority wills" is by no means identical with the proposition "the majority always wills that which is right," the two propositions nevertheless come to precisely the same thing when considered as first principles of politics—since it follows from both that a good political system is one which lodges ultimate power in the hands of the majority.

The first proposition is not identical with the second because, *when it stands by itself*, it does involve an uncompromising relativism about right and wrong (*i.e.*, it involves a theory regarding the nature of right), while the second, involving as it does merely a judgment regarding the quantitative relation between the wise and the just, on the one hand, and the foolish and the unjust on the other hand, can keep house quite comfortably with the belief that there are moral standards which do not in any sense depend for their validity upon acceptance by majorities. The second, in a word, is completely free of the suggestion that the majority will is right because it is the majority's.

But so also is the *first* proposition free of that suggestion when it is put forward as a corollary of the second—*i.e.*, when it is urged by a writer who can be shown to believe the second proposition and to believe in the existence of objective moral standards. For the writer who believes that there are objective moral standards and that the majority of each political society both accept and know how to apply these standards can say that what the majority wills is right without committing himself to the idea that what the minority wills is wrong *because* it is willed by a minority. He can, too, easily slip into the habit of asserting that what the majority wills is right without reminding his readers that he intends nothing more than a judgment regarding the moral capacity of majorities.

Now Locke, together, perhaps, with most of the majority-rule demo-crats, did believe (as we have seen in the opening sections of this chapter) in the existence of objective moral standards, and he did reveal, in several passages of the *Second Treatise,* a conviction that the majority of any commonwealth can be trusted, not only to arrive at and fight for and impose its will, but to arrive at and fight for and impose a *right* will. He never, to be sure, actually says that he believes this,[5] but there are passages in the *Second Treatise* which are intelligible only on the hypoth-esis that he did.[6] The king who violates the written law in obedience to the maxim *salus populi suprema lex,* "cannot miss the consent and appro-bation of the community."[7] It is not true that the people are ignorant and perpetually discontented, their opinion "unsteady" and their humor "uncertain."[8] The people are not to be blamed if they "have the sense of rational creatures."[9] The people are not "void of reason and brutish."[10] The people know when the treatment they are receiving is "contrary to right," and do not lack the courage to resist the government from which they receive such treatment.[11] The evidence is not conclusive, but it does suggest that Locke would have subscribed to the proposition that a "safe" majority of men (thus the "average" man) are rational and just.[12]

It is, in this background, instructive to ask oneself the following ques-tion: If Locke had written across the top of the first page of the *Second Treatise* the words, "All theoretical demonstrations included in the fol-lowing argument are predicated upon the assumption that the chances are at least 50+ out of 100 that the average man is rational and just," would we (assuming the validity of the predication) need to withdraw any of the criticisms which we have brought against Locke's political system? The correct answer is, in this writer's opinion, that most of the diffi-culties to which we have directed attention above would automatically disappear. The man who thinks he knows that the majority is rational and just can speak of the right of the majority and remain silent about the duties which attach to that right, because it follows as a matter of course from his major premise that the latter will be discharged. He can equate

---

[5]Cf. Locke, *ap.* Peter King King, *The Life and Letters of John Locke* (London: Bell & Daldy, 1864), p. 283: "Every man knows in those few cases which concern his own actions what is right and what is wrong."
[6]Cf. Lamprecht, *op. cit.,* p. 22: "[Locke] stood so close to the deists that he has some-times been classified as one of their number." Cf. *ibid.,* pp. 28-29: "Their [the deists'] com-placently optimistic estimate of man's naturally moral character is most extravagant . . . . Probably it was just the equivocations in the thought of the deists which were partly re-sponsible for Locke's wavering and unsettled explanation of the foundations of the moral law."
[7]xiii. 158.
[8]xix. 223.
[9]xix. 230.
[10]xiv. 163.
[11]xix. 224.
[12]Although he was quite capable of arguing the contrary when it served his purpose. Cf. ix. 123, where he is of the opinion that the greater part of men are "no strict observers of equity and justice." Cf. ix. 125, where he is of the opinion that men are "partial to themselves," thus not to be trusted as judges in their own cases. Cf. ix. 124: "Men, being biased by their interest, as well as ignorant for want of study [of the law of nature], ... are not apt to allow of it as a law binding to them."

the good of each nation-state with the good of mankind, because the good of a nation-state controlled by the majority of its people would, on his showing, be the good of mankind. He can argue both for individual rights and for a right in the majority to define individual rights because the kind of majority he has in mind would never withdraw a right which the individual ought to have. He can overlook the necessity for careful definition of the public good, because on his showing the majority of each society will (if their institutions enable them to influence the course of events) prevent the "forces" of the society from being used for any purpose other than the promotion of the rational and just; and the individual's duty to obey the majority follows as a matter of course from his duty to promote the rational and just. The individual can, in his view, covenant to obey the majority without subjecting himself to the absolute and arbitrary authority of other persons, since the judgments of the majority are those of reason and justice.[13] In short, Locke's doctrine of majority-rule becomes a series of identical propositions the moment we attribute to it such a latent premise as the above, and, on any other premise, must be dismissed as highly extravagant ethical nonsense.[14] And if this is true, then the issue posed by the *Second Treatise* is simply whether or not the figure 50+ in the above estimate of probability is or is not accurate, and, if it is inaccurate, in which direction? No one, probably, would insist upon the figure 100, and no one on the figure 0, and though the wise man would refuse to name a figure at all, it may well be that our views upon the vexed problem of majority-rule necessarily involve a (perhaps unconscious) judgment as to whether the correct figure is more or less than 50—as (*e.g.*) our selection of a wardrobe for a week-end in the country involves a (perhaps unconscious) judgment as to the probable behavior of the weather.

The capital weakness of Locke's *Second Treatise* is to be sought in its author's failure to assign to this central issue the prominence which it deserves, and to raise the question, How can we *test* the unconscious judgments regarding the incidence of rationality and justice in human nature which reveal themselves in our attitude towards the proposals of the majority-rule democrats, in order to free our thought from its

---

[13]Cf. John Locke, *Thoughts Concerning Education* (London: Printed for J. and R. Tonson, 1769), p. 61: "Though [reputation] be not the true principle and measure of virtue, ... it is that which comes nearest to it."

[14]That is, unless one be willing to make this act of faith, one will be well advised to abandon the notion of a majority-right to conclude the minority. It is not enough to assert, with Croce (*Storia d'Italia dal 1871 al 1915* [Bari: Laterza & Figli, 1928], p. 9), that "non si è trovato finora altro modo di educare i popoli alla libertà, cioè di educarli senz' altro, che quello di concedere loro la libertà e di far che imparino con l'esperienza, e magari col fiaccarsi la testa." Croce cites Ferdinando Martini (*Due dell' Estrema—Il Guerrazzi e il Brofferio* [Firenze Le Monnier, 1920], p. ix) to the effect that the "moderates," *i.e.*, those who are unwilling to see peoples actually use the liberty which the democratic movement professes to offer them, are like a parent who, "regalato a' figlioli un tamburo, li ammonisce che si divertano ma non facciano rumore." The comparison is an amusing one; but peoples often get their hands on more dangerous playthings than drums, and unless there be a presumption that they will use them well, how are we to answer the man (*e.g.*, Jellinek) who thinks they will be better off without them?

dependence upon uncriticized generalizations founded upon our own limited experience as individuals? Whether or not a premise similar to Locke's *does* underlie the thought of more recent majority-rule democrats,[15] and whether it remains, with them as with Locke, merely latent, are problems which must be postponed to a later phase of the investigation of which the study which we here conclude is but the first stage.

---

[15]Cf. F. J. C. Hearnshaw, *Democracy and the British Empire* (London: Constable & Co., 1920), p. 201: "The faith of a democrat [in our terminology, "majority-rule democrat"] requires him to believe that in the long run the majority of the people finds its way to the truth, and that in the long run it tries to do the right." Cf. Lerner, *op. cit.*, p. 107: "My own conviction [is] that the majority in a state represents a good bet in the long pull of history."

BIBLIOGRAPHY OF WORKS CITED

AARON, R. I., *John Locke.* London: Oxford University Press, 1937.
ADAMS, HENRY, *The Degradation of the Democratic Dogma,* with an Introduction by Brooks Adams. New York: The Macmillan Co., 1919.
ALLEN, J. W., *A History of Political Thought in the Sixteenth Century.* London: Methuen & Co., 1928.
ALLPORT, FLOYD HENRY, *Institutional Behavior.* Chapel Hill: University of North Carolina Press, 1933.
ALTHUSIUS, JOHANNES, *Politica methodice digesta,* edited with an Introduction by Carl Joachim Friedrich. Cambridge: Harvard University Press, 1932.
ARISTOTLE, *Works,* translated into English under the editorship of W. D. Ross. Vol. X, 1: *Politica,* by Benjamin Jowett. Revised edition, Oxford: Clarendon Press, 1921.
BARCLAY, WILLIAM, *De regno et regali potestate.* Parisiis: Apud G. Chaudière, 1600.
BERLE, ADOLPH A., and GARDINER C. MEANS, *The Modern Corporation and Private Property.* New York: The Macmillan Co., 1934.
BLACKMUR, R. P., "Henry and Brooks Adams," *The Southern Review,* V (1939), pp. 308-334.
BLACKSTONE, SIR WILLIAM, *Commentaries on the Laws of England.* Philadelphia: J. B. Lippincott & Co., 2 vols., 1859.
BODIN, JEAN, *Les six livres de la Republique.* Paris: Chez Jacques du Puys, 1577.
BOUDIN, LOUIS B., *Government by Judiciary.* New York: William Godwin, 2 vols., 1932.
BRADLEY, F. H., *Ethical Studies.* London: Henry S. King & Co., 1876.
BRIERLY, J. L., *The Law of Nations: An Introduction to the International Law of Peace.* Oxford: Clarendon Press, 1936.
BUCHANAN, GEORGE, *Opera omnia,* edidit Thomas Ruddimannus. Edinburgi: Apud Robertum Freebairn, 1715.
BURKE, EDMUND, *Works.* Vol. III, *An Appeal from the New to the Old Whigs.* London: Henry G. Bohn, 1855.
————, *Reflections on the French Revolution.* London: J. M. Dent & Sons, 1910.
BURNS, G. DESLISLE, *Political Ideals.* London: Oxford University Press, 1927.
CAIRNES, HUNTINGTON, *Law and the Social Sciences.* New York: Harcourt, Brace & Co., 1935.
CARPENTER, WILLIAM SEAL, *The Development of American Political Thought.* Princeton: Princeton University Press, 1930.
————, *v.s.v.* Locke.
CARRITT, E. A., *The Theory of Morals.* Oxford: University Press, 1928.
————, *Morals and Politics.* Oxford: University Press, 1935.
CATLIN, G. E. G., *The Science and Method of Politics.* London: Kegan Paul, Trench, Trubner & Co., 1927.
————, *Principles of Politics.* New York: The Macmillan Co., 1930.
————, *The Story of the Political Philosophers.* New York: McGraw-Hill Book Co., 1939.
COHEN, MORRIS R., *Reason and Nature: An Essay on the Meaning of Scientific Method.* New York: Harcourt, Brace & Co., 1931.
COLE, G. D. H., *Social Theory.* London: Methuen & Co., 1920.
————, *v.s.v.* Rousseau.
CROCE, BENEDETTO, *Storia d'Italia dal 1871 al 1915.* Bari: Laterza & Figli, 1928.
DALBERG-ACTON, JOHN EMERICH EDWARD, *The History of Freedom and Other Essays,* edited by John Neville Figgis and Reginald Vere Laurence. London: Macmillan & Co., 1907.

DENNIS, LAWRENCE, *The Dynamics of War and Revolution.* New York: The Weekly Foreign Letter, 1940.

DICEY, A. V., *The Law of the Constitution.* London: Macmillan & Co., 1927.

DIONYSIUS OF HALICARNASSUS, *Antiquitatum Romanarum* quae supersunt, Graece et Latine ex recensione Adolphi Kiessling et Victoris Prou. Parisiis: Editoribus Firmin Didot et Sociis, 1876.

DUNNING, WILLIAM ARCHIBALD, *A History of Political Theories from Luther to Montesquieu.* New York and London: The Macmillan Co., 1905.

ELLIOTT, EDWARD, *American Government and Majority Rule.* Princeton: Princeton University Press, 1916.

ESMEIN, A., *Éléments de droit constitutionnel français et comparé.* 4ᵉ ed., Paris: Librairie J. B. Sirey, 1906.

FEIBELMAN, JAMES, *Positive Democracy.* Chapel Hill: University of North Carolina Press, 1940.

FIGGIS, JOHN NEVILLE, *The Divine Right of Kings.* Cambridge: University Press, 1914.

FINER, HERMAN, *The Theory and Practice of Modern Government.* London: Methuen & Co., 2 vols., 1932.

FRASER, A. CAMPBELL, "John Locke as a Factor in Modern Thought," *Proceedings of the British Academy,* 1903-1904, pp. 221-235.

FRIEDRICH, CARL JOACHIM, *Constitutional Government and Politics: Nature and Development.* New York: Harper & Bros., 1937.

————, "One Majority Against Another," *The Southern Review,* V (1939), pp. 42-52.

————, *v.s.v.* Althusius.

GIERKE, OTTO VON, *Das deutsche Genossenschaftsrecht.* Berlin: Weidmann, 4 vols., 1868-1913.

————, *Johannes Althusius und die Entwicklung der naturrechtlichen Staatstheorien.* Breslau: M. & H. Marcus, 1902.

————, *The Development of Political Theory,* translated by Bernard Freyd. New York: W. W. Norton & Co., 1939.

————, "Über die Geschichte des Majoritätsprinzipes," *Schmollers Jahrbuch für Gesetzgebung Verwaltung und Volkswirtschaft im Deutschen Reiche,* XXXIX (1915), pp. 565-587.

GOOCH, G. P., *English Democratic Ideas in the Seventeenth Century.* 2d edition, Cambridge: University Press, 1927.

GREEN, THOMAS HILL, *Lectures on the Principles of Political Obligation.* London: Longmans, Green, & Co., 1917.

GRIMKE, FREDERICK, *Considerations upon the Nature and Tendency of Free Institutions.* 2d edition, New York: Derby & Jackson, 1856.

GROTIUS, HUGO, *De iure belli ac pacis libri tres* cum annotatis auctoris, edidit P. C. Molhuysen. Lugduni Batavorum: Apud A. W. Sijthoff, 1919.

GUICCIARDINI, FRANCESCO, *Ricordi politici e civili,* a cura di Pietro Pancrazi. Firenze: Rinascimento del libro, 1929.

HARRINGTON, JAMES, *Oceana.* Heidelberg: C. Winter, 1924.

HEARNSHAW, F. J. C., *Democracy and the British Empire.* London: Constable & Co., 1920.

HEIMANN, EDUARD, *Communism, Fascism or Democracy?* New York: W. W. Norton & Co., 1938.

HEINBERG, J. G., "Theories of Majority Rule," *American Political Science Review,* XXVI (June, 1932), pp. 452-469.

HENDEL, CHARLES WILLIAM, *Jean-Jacques Rousseau, Moralist.* London: Oxford University Press, 2 vols., 1934.

HOBBES, THOMAS, *Elementa philosophica de cive.* Amsterodami: Apud L. & D. Elzevirios, 1657.

————, *Leviathan.* London: J. M. Dent & Sons, 1914.

HOLLAND, T. E., *The Elements of Jurisprudence.* 13th edition, Oxford: The Clarendon Press, 1924.

HOOK, SIDNEY, "Reflections on the Russian Revolution," *The Southern Review*, IV (1939), pp. 429-462.
————, "The Integral Humanism of Jacques Maritain," *Partisan Review*, VII (1940), pp. 204-229.
HOPKINS, WILLIAM L., "The Framework for the Use of Labor," *Annals of the American Academy of Political and Social Science*, CCVI (November, 1939), pp. 42-46.
HOTMAN, FRANÇOIS, *Franco-Gallia seu Tractatus isagogicus de regimina regum Galliae et de jure successionis*. Coloniae: Ex officina J. Bertulphi, 1576.
JAMES I, *Political Works*, edited with an Introduction by Charles H. McIlwain. Cambridge: Harvard University Press, 1918.
JELLINEK, GEORG, *Das Recht der Minoritäten*. Wien: Alfred Hölder, 1898.
JOËL, KARL, *Wandlungen der Weltanschauung*. Tübingen: Propyläen Verlag, 2 vols., 1928-1934.
"JUNIUS BRUTUS," *A Defence of Liberty Against Tyrants*, with an Introduction by Harold J. Laski. London: G. Bell & Sons, 1924.
KALES, ALBERT M., *Unpopular Government in the United States*. Chicago: University of Chicago Press, 1914.
KEIR, D. L., *The Constitutional History of Modern Britain 1485-1937*. New York: D. Van Nostrand Co., 1938.
KENDALL, WILLMOORE, "The Majority Principle and the Scientific Elite," *The Southern Review*, IV (1939), pp. 463-473.
KEYNES, J. M., *A Treatise on Money*. London: Macmillan & Co., 2 vols., 1930.
KING, PETER KING, *The Life and Letters of John Locke*, with extracts from his journals and commonplace books. London: Bell & Daldy, 1864.
KIZEVETTER, A., "Travaux des savants russes émigrés (1918-1928)," *Revue historique*, CLXIII (1930), pp. 160-183.
KNOX, JOHN, *Works*, edited by David Laing. Edinburg: For the Bannatyne Club, 6 vols., 1844-1846.
KONOPCZYŃSKI, LADISLAS, "Majority Rule," *Encyclopaedia of the Social Sciences*. New York: The Macmillan Co., Vol. X, 1933.
KRABBE, H., *Die moderne Staats-idee*. Haag: Martinus Nijhoff, 1919.
————, *The Modern Idea of the State*, translated with an Introduction by George H. Sabine and Walter J. Shepard. New York: D. Appleton & Co., 1922.
LAMPRECHT, STERLING POWER, *The Moral and Political Philosophy of John Locke*. New York: Columbia University Press, 1918.
————, "Hobbes and Hobbism," *American Political Science Review*, XXXIV (February, 1940), pp. 31-53.
LANGUET, HUBERT, *v.s.v.* "Junius Brutus."
LASKI, HAROLD J., *Authority in the Modern State*. New Haven: Yale University Press, 1919.
————, *A Grammar of Politics*. London: George Allen & Unwin, 1928.
————, *Democracy in Crisis*. London: George Allen & Unwin, 1934.
————, *The Rise of Liberalism*. New York: Harper & Bros., 1936.
————, *Parliamentary Government in England: a Commentary*. New York: Viking Press, 1938.
LERNER, MAX, *It Is Later Than You Think: The Need for a Militant Democracy*. New York: Viking Press, 1938.
LOCKE, JOHN, *Two Treatises of Government*. London: For Awnsham Churchill, 1690.
————, *Some Thoughts Concerning Education*. London: For J. & R. Tonson, 1769.
————, *Essay Concerning Human Understanding*. Edited by A. C. Fraser. Oxford: University Press, 2 vols., 1894.
————, *Of Civil Government*, with an Introduction by William S. Carpenter. London: J. M. Dent & Sons, 1936.

LORD, ARTHUR RITCHIE, *The Principles of Politics.* Oxford: Clarendon Press, 1921.
MCILWAIN, C. H., *The Growth of Political Thought in the West.* New York: The Macmillan Co., 1932.
————, *v.s.v.* James I.
MACIVER, R. M., *Community: A Sociological Study.* London: Macmillan and Co., 1920.
————, *Leviathan and the People.* Baton Rouge: Louisiana State University Press, 1939.
MACHIAVELLI, NICCOLÒ, *Tutte le opere,* a cura di G. Massoni e M. Casella. Firenze: G. Barbèra, 1929.
MARIANA, JUAN DE, *De rege et regis institutione libri tres.* Toleti: P. Rodericus, 1599.
MARSILIUS OF PADUA, *Defensor pacis.* Leipzig und Berlin: Verlag von B. G. Teubner, 1914.
————, *Defensor pacis,* edited by C. W. Previté-Orton. Cambridge: University Press, 1928.
MARTIN, EVERETT DEAN, "The Place of Government in Modern Economic Society," *Annals of the American Academy of Political and Social Science,* CCVI (November, 1939), pp. 12-16.
MARTINI, FERDINANDO, *Due dell'Estrema—Il Guerrazzi e il Brofferio,* Carteggi inediti 1859-1866. Firenze: Le Monnier, 1920.
MEANS, GARDINER C., *v.s.v.* A. Berle.
MÉRAY, C. H. VON, *Weltmutation.* Zürich: Max Rascher, 1918.
MILTON, JOHN, *Prose Works,* edited by J. A. St. John. London: George Bell & Sons, 6 vols., 1904-1909.
MIRABEAU, HONORÉ GABRIEL RIQUETTI, *Œuvres.* Paris: Lecointe et Pougin, Vol. I, 1834.
D'ORS, EUGENIO, "Métahistoire," *Revue des questions historiques,* Mars 1934 *et seqq.*
PARRINGTON, VERNON LOUIS, *Main Currents in American Thought:* An Interpretation of American Literature from the Beginnings to 1920. New York: Harcourt, Brace and Co., 3 vols., 1927.
PETCH, JAMES A., *v.s.v.* "Xenophon."
PLATO, *The Dialogues,* translated by B. Jowett. 2d edition, 5 vols., Oxford: Clarendon Press, 1875.
————, *The Republic,* edited with an English translation by Paul Shorey. London: William Heinemann, 2 vols., 1930-1935.
PLINY THE YOUNGER, *Epistularum libri decem,* recensuit Elmer Truesdell Merill. Lipsiae: In aedibus B. G. Teubneri, 1922.
PÖHLMANN, R. VON, *Geschichte der sozialen Frage und des Sozialismus in der antiken Welt,* edited by Friedrich Oertel. München: Beck'sche Verlagsbuchhandlung, 1925.
POLLOCK, SIR FREDERICK, "Locke's Theory of the State," *Proceedings of the British Academy,* 1903-1904, pp. 237-249.
PREVITÉ-ORTON, *v.s.v.* Marsilius.
PUFENDORF, SAMUEL VON, *De officio hominis et civis juxta legem naturalem libri duo.* New York. Oxford University Press, 1927.
————, *De iure naturae et gentium libri octo.* Oxford: The Clarendon Press, 1934.
RAVEN, ALEXANDER, *Civilization as Divine Superman.* London: Williams & Norgate, 1932.
REYNOLDS, BEATRICE, *Proponents of Limited Monarchy in Sixteenth Century France.* New York: Columbia University Press, 1931.
RITCHIE, DAVID G., *Natural Rights: A Criticism of Some Political and Ethical Conceptions.* London: Swan Sonnenschein & Co., 1895.
ROUSSEAU, JEAN-JACQUES, *Œuvres complètes,* avec des éclaircissements par V. D. Musset-Pathay. Paris: Chez P. Dupont, 23 vols., 1823-1826.

————, *Du contrat social*. Édition comprenant avec le texte définitif les versions primitives de l'ouvrage collationnées sur les manuscrits autographes de Genève et de Neuchâtel, avec une introduction et des notes, par Edmond Dreyfus-Brisac. Paris: Félix Alcan, 1896.

————, *The Social Contract and Discourses*, with an Introduction by G. D. H. Cole. London: J. M. Dent & Sons, 1913.

————, *The Political Writings*, edited with introductions and notes by Charles Edwyn Vaughan. Cambridge: University Press, 1915.

RUFFINI AVONDO, EDOARDO, *Il principio maggioritario: Profilo storico*. Torino: Fratelli Bocca, 1927.

————, "Il principio maggioritario nella storia del diritto cononico," *Archivio giuridico*, XCIII (1925), pp. 15-67.

RUSSELL, BERTRAND, *Power, a New Social Analysis*. New York: W. W. Norton & Co., 1938.

SABINE, GEORGE H., *A History of Political Theory*. New York: Henry Holt & Co., 1937.

————, *v.s.v.* Krabbe.

SARIPOLOS, NICOLAS, *La démocratie et l'élection proportionelle: Étude historique, juridique, et politique*. Paris: Arthur Rousseau, 1899.

SHEPARD, WALTER J., *v.s.v.* Krabbe.

SIEYÈS, EMMANUEL JOSEPH, COMTE, *Qu'est-ce que le tiers état?* Précédé de *l'Essai sur les privilèges*. Paris: A. Coreard, 1822.

SIMMEL, GEORG, *Soziologie: Untersuchungen über die Formen der Vergesellschaftungen*. Leipzig: Duncker & Humblot, 1908.

SIMONDE DE SISMONDI, J. C. L., *Études sur les constitutions des peuples libres*. Paris: Treuttel et Würtz, 1836.

SMITH, J. ALLEN, *The Spirit of American Government*. New York: The Macmillan Co., 1912.

————, *The Growth and Decadence of Constitutional Government*. New York: Henry Holt & Co., 1930.

SOROKIN, PITIRIM A., *Social and Cultural Dynamics*. New York: The Macmillan Co., 3 vols., 1936-1938.

SPENGLER, OSWALD, *The Decline of the West,* translated by Charles F. Atkinson. New York: Alfred A. Knopf, 2 vols., 1928.

STAROSOLSKYJ, WOLODYMYR, *Das Majoritätsprinzip*. (Wiener Staatswissenschaftliche Studien, Vol. XIII, 2.) Wien und Leipzig: F. Deuticke, 1916.

STAWSKI, JOSEPH, *Le principe de la majorité (son histoire, son fondement, et les limites de son application): étude sur la formation de la volonté collective dans le domaine politique*. Gedani: Ex Officina Boenigiana, 1920.

STORY, JOSEPH, *Commentaries on the Constitution*. 3d edition, Boston: Little, Brown & Co., 2 vols., 1858.

STUDEBAKER, JOHN WARD, *Plain Talk*. Washington: National Home Library Association, 1936.

SWABEY, MARIE COLLINS, *Theory of the Democratic State*. Cambridge: Harvard University Press, 1937.

THUCYDIDES, translated into English with introduction and notes by B. Jowett. 2 vols., Oxford: Clarendon Press, 1881.

TOYNBEE, ARNOLD J., *A Study of History*. London: Oxford Press, 6 vols., 1934-1939.

VAUGHAN, C. E., *Studies in the History of Political Philosophy before and after Rousseau,* edited by A. G. Little. Manchester: University Press, 2 vols., 1925.

————, *v.s.v.* Rousseau.

WILLIAMS, ALFRED TUTTLE, *The Concept of Equality in the Writings of Rousseau, Bentham, and Kant*. New York: Teachers College, Columbia University, 1907.

WILSON, FRANCIS G., *Elements of Modern Politics*. New York: McGraw-Hill Book Co., 1936.

"XENOPHON," *The Old Oligarch*. Translated with an Introduction by James A. Petch. Oxford: University Press, 1926.